LAW SCHOOL SUCCESS

LAW SCHOOL SUCCESS

❖

Advice from a Law Professor

Learn Law Better, LLC

H. BEAU BAEZ, LAW PROFESSOR

ISBN-13: 978-0-9861455-2-0 (soft cover book)

ISBN-13: 978-0-9861455-3-7 (eBook)

ISBN-13: 978-0-9861455-4-4 (audiobook)

Published in the United States by Learn Law Better, LLC

LearnLawBetter.com

First Edition

For Jenny, who has helped me on my journey—*semper fidelis*

TABLE OF CONTENTS

FIGURES

INTRODUCTION

I chose to go to law school because I thought that someday, somehow, I'd make a difference.

CHRISTOPHER DARDEN

This book is designed to help students succeed in law school. Regardless of which law school you attend, you must develop new skills and significantly improve those you already have. Included here are techniques, methods, and approaches to studying law I have found most successful with the thousands of law students I have taught in the classroom or tutored online at many different law schools, including Harvard, Chicago, and Georgetown. More important than personal observation, the skills learned here are primarily based on scientifically validated research, which should help improve your learning outcomes.

Before reading any further, it is important to understand a few things about this book and legal education. First and foremost, reading and implementing these strategies are not a guarantee to earning the highest grades in law school—no book, course, or person can honestly make that promise. Second, not everyone begins law school with the same knowledge, skills, and abilities—some start with a few academic advantages based on their past experiences, such as having attended a highly ranked preparatory school with a world-class writing program. These strategies, however, can help narrow the gap, improving the potential for success. Third, success requires investing time and effort, which often corresponds to sixty hours or more a week dedicated to law school. Fourth, not everything in this book will work for everyone, but I recommend trying a new strategy before rejecting it. Finally, this book's primary focus is to improve exam performance within the context of the time constraints experienced by most law students.

The advice in this book attempts to provide a path between the ideal and the practical, providing guidance on what realistically can be accomplished in a day. Assuming three classes a day, that works out to four hours in class, two hours reviewing, four hours preparing for the next day's classes, and personal time for meals, commutes, brief conversations with colleagues, and sleep. Given these realities, this book takes a pragmatic view of law school, providing recommendations that most law students can achieve with the amount of time they have.

Law school is challenging because, maybe for the first time in your life, you are surrounded by classmates who are as bright as or brighter than you—the proverbial small fish in a big pond. Everyone is working hard to earn the best grades, which are awarded to only a few students because strict grading curves limit the professor's latitude to assign top grades. The law school's mandatory grading system means students aren't measured by their individual performance but rather by their performance relative to their classmates. Hard work and effort don't guarantee success, and the techniques that worked well in college are practically useless in law school. To get to the top of the class it is essential to develop new study strategies, time management techniques, and self-discipline.

The most common mistake for first-year law students is their focus on mastering legal doctrine. Knowledge acquisition worked well in the past but is almost useless in law school. While learning the law is necessary, more important is developing better study techniques and mastering the law school exam. In college, most students read their assignments, take notes in class, and then cram right before finals—cramming remains a common study strategy.[1] And when course material isn't easily understood, many reread the same material until it's mastered. That approach does not work in law school for several reasons. First, the amount of reading and legal terminology is overwhelming. Second, there are better methods that result in deeper learning. And third, it is essential to make time for daily review and outline creation, which helps with learning and exam preparation. Learning these new skills helps in becoming a better student and a better lawyer.

In preparing this book, I reviewed nearly one hundred "law school success" books written over the past thirty years. Almost all of them are actually "law school orientation" books, which preview first-year courses, explain how case law is used, discuss statutes, introduce the legal system, and otherwise provide a broad overview on what to expect in law school. Unfortunately, these books tend to discuss only a few skills essential for success, generally case briefing and how to use the IRAC exam writing method. This book is different because it focuses on the broader range of skills needed to succeed rather than on the inner workings of law school life. I should note that law school orientation books are valuable because they help demystify the law school experience, but I chose not to include that material here because it would have added 200 pages to the book. More importantly though, it would have shifted attention from skills development, which ultimately is the foundation for strong study habits and better grades.

Finally, this book is designed for the student who is willing to become uncomfortable and develop new skills. At first, these techniques will be hard to master and feel counterintuitive. This is true anytime someone begins mastering something new. By way of illustration, when I decided to go on a 100-mile backpacking trip, one of my first purchases was an expensive pair of hiking boots. My prior lifetime experience of purchasing shoes was practically worthless, though I didn't know that until I went on my first hike. At first, I thought I just needed to break in the new shoes, but after each hike my feet were in pain. I then thought I had purchased the wrong brand, so I went to a store for hikers to purchase something better. A store employee—an experienced hiker—explained the technical aspect of how the shoe and foot interact when hiking, revealing the secret to better hiking shoes: purchase hiking shoes that are one size larger than you normally get. I was incredulous. After all, I had been buying shoes for nearly forty years—I knew my shoe size. Reluctantly, I purchased the larger hiking shoes. And just like that, my feet were fine. I had a great two-week backpacking trip and years of enjoyable mountain hiking. This wouldn't have happened unless I had been willing to talk to an expert, challenge my assumptions, and follow the advice of the more experienced.

When you start law school, you won't appreciate your skills deficit until after the semester is over because most professors provide only one final exam. By that point it may be too late to get into the top of the class or, for some, avoid academic dismissal. This means making changes to old study routines from day one. Also, swallow your pride and follow the advice. There are many who believe the tools that worked well for them in college will propel them to success in law school—they won't. Many learn this lesson only after they get their first grades, by which time their law school grade point average is irreparably harmed.

This book is divided into three sections, with the first part of the book focusing on essential study skills. This includes understanding cases, study aids, and the Socratic Method and developing new skills to get you through your classes and on to your exams. The second part focuses on law school exams and a few advanced skills to help you succeed. While a thorough discussion of exam techniques is beyond the scope of this book, you will learn what law school exams are like so you can begin preparing for exams from day one of law school. The third part of the book involves life's greatest challenge: the inward journey. This is where you learn more about time management, procrastination, substance abuse, mindfulness, and other internal challenges that keep you from reaching your highest potential in law school and beyond. One final note concerning language: There are points in the book where ideas are repeated. This is intentional. Some concepts are so important that they are presented more than once for emphasis.

HOW TO USE THIS BOOK

Unfortunately, the very methods that served law students well in the past will guarantee their failure in law school.

RUTA K. STROPUS

E ach chapter begins by discussing an issue or problem faced in law school. Ideally, follow that advice. However, when there isn't enough time in the day, sometimes you will see a "second-best" section. But when you take the second-best approach, consider mixing it up with the primary advice when possible.

The book also provides Student Story and Brain Insight sections, which provide background to the discussion in the chapter. These sections are not essential to developing the skills needed in law school but can help with understanding why they are important. Finally, some sections have exercises, which can be used for developing the skills needed for success.

The Student Story sections are actual stories from law students with whom I have worked at nearly a hundred law schools primarily in the United States but also in Australia, Canada, and the United Kingdom. To protect their privacy, I do not use real names, and some details have been changed.

The Brain Insight section explains the cognitive science behind the recommended approaches and techniques. This can be helpful for those who are interested in cognitive science or maybe have a healthy skepticism towards learning a new technique. Or maybe you received advice from a video, book, or law student that is different from what you find here. By understanding the science, you may be more comfortable with implementing a new strategy, which is essential to learning and exam preparation.

Finally, this book contains more techniques and strategies that can be employed all at once. If a technique isn't working for you, that's okay. Law school is a marathon, not a sprint. This means building learning competencies a few at a time. Feel free to look at the table of contents and find a section that catches your attention. And periodically during your law school journey, come back and begin using a new technique—the goal is continuous improvement.

PART I:
ESSENTIAL SKILLS

Tell me, and I forget; teach me, and I remember;
involve me, and I learn.

XUNZI, CHINESE PHILOSOPHER

Learning new skills, or improving old ones, is essential to law school success. When we were children, education focused almost exclusively on retaining knowledge—learning the alphabet, new vocabulary, names of important historical figures, the nation's capital, and so on. Remembering is the first and lowest form of learning, and as a child you spent the most time developing these cognitive abilities. After remembering, the next step was learning to understand what those facts meant, like understanding that letters make up words and words comprise sentences. Legal education, just like every other discipline, requires the comprehension of vast amounts of new knowledge, but, unlike prior education, students are required to move beyond remembering and understanding to the higher thinking domains of application, analysis, evaluation, and creation. This is where new tools are needed to succeed. Also, because law school demands lots of time—60 hours a week for most law students—it is necessary to improve on the study techniques developed in high school and college.

In 1956, Benjamin Bloom published a learning hierarchy, today called "Bloom's Taxonomy." It provides a visual ordering of cognitive skills, with remembering at the base and then moving upwards through the more complex learning domains. While there is some overlap between each domain, you must generally employ different study techniques at each level. By grasping how learning progresses and the cognitive levels assessed on a law school exam, you can focus on developing the right skills for each type of thinking and then spend some time working on skills appropriate to each level. To illustrate, flashcards are an effective tool for remembering, less useful for understanding, and practically worthless for all the other, higher-level domains. As discussed in more detail later, you need to spend time on remembering and understanding, but to do well on law school exams you must also spend time developing the skills of applying, analyzing, evaluating, and, to a lesser degree, creating.

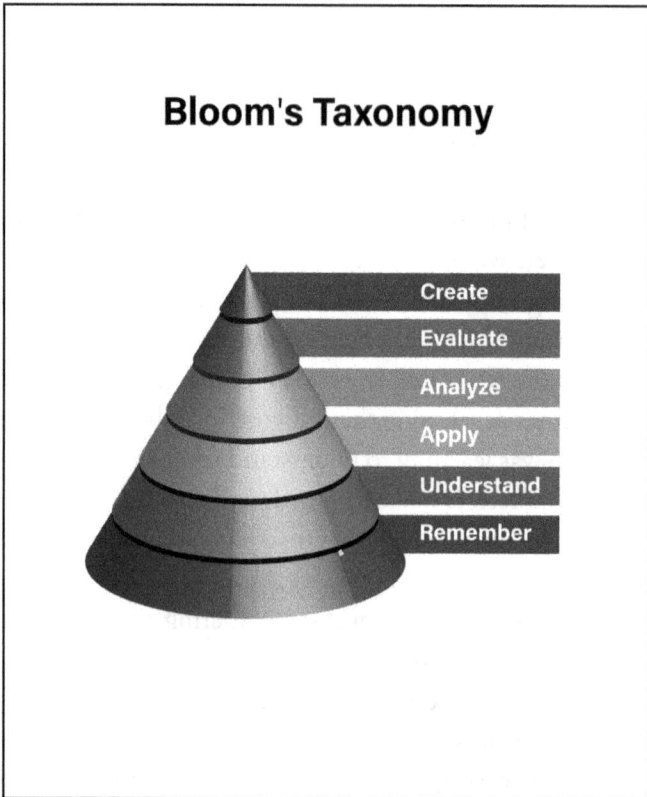

Bloom's Taxonomy

Create
Evaluate
Analyze
Apply
Understand
Remember

To achieve success in law school, it is crucial to understand the ideal way to master new knowledge. Take for example, one of the more difficult topics in the first-year law school curriculum: the rule against perpetuities, which is taught in many property law courses and appears on the bar exam. Before the class when the rule is discussed, most students follow the *Common Study Cycle*™. This approach worked well before law school, so you begin by reading the assigned material and possibly a commercial study aid. At first, the definition for the rule against perpetuities makes sense, or so you think: "No interest is good unless it must vest, if at all, not later than 21 years after some life in being at the creation of the interest." There is a level of comprehension and understanding before going to class. During class, the professor begins discussing hypotheticals for a "life in being," including a question on what happens when Dad leaves real estate to Kyle in his will for Kyle's life and then to Kyle's children when they turn 23. The class assumes the will does not violate the rule against perpetuities because Kyle is a life in being. But because Kyle is alive and could theoretically have a child years after Dad dies, this attempt by Dad to give assets to someone 21 years beyond a life in being invalidates the will. Then the professor mentions the possibility of the fertile octogenarian—yes, a real term discussed in law school—and there is more confusion. They hear example after example from the professor, and finally everyone leaves mentally exhausted.

After class, preparation for the next day's reading begins, and most students defer really learning the rule against perpetuities until the end of the semester. During college, many students prepare for final exams by spending a few days cramming just before finals, so in law school many fall back on this strategy. But this is unlikely to work in law school, especially with concepts that many lawyers and judges don't fully grasp even after years of practice. During the rush before finals, many students review their notes, prepare a study outline, or purchase a commercial outline for the course. After a few weeks of reading, cramming, and enduring sleepless nights, the final exam is over. Very little of what this student learned during the semester was ever moved into long-term memory, resulting in less-than-stellar grades and requiring the student to cram three years later for the bar exam. There is a better way.

Mastering vast amounts of legal knowledge requires a different approach to studying. Knowledge gained in law school, if properly stored in long-term memory, can be accessed not only on course exams but also on the bar exam and then years later during the practice of law. Many students fail the bar exam because they used the *Common Study Cycle*™ during law school, which got them through law school but not beyond the bar exam. There is a strong correlation between first-year law school

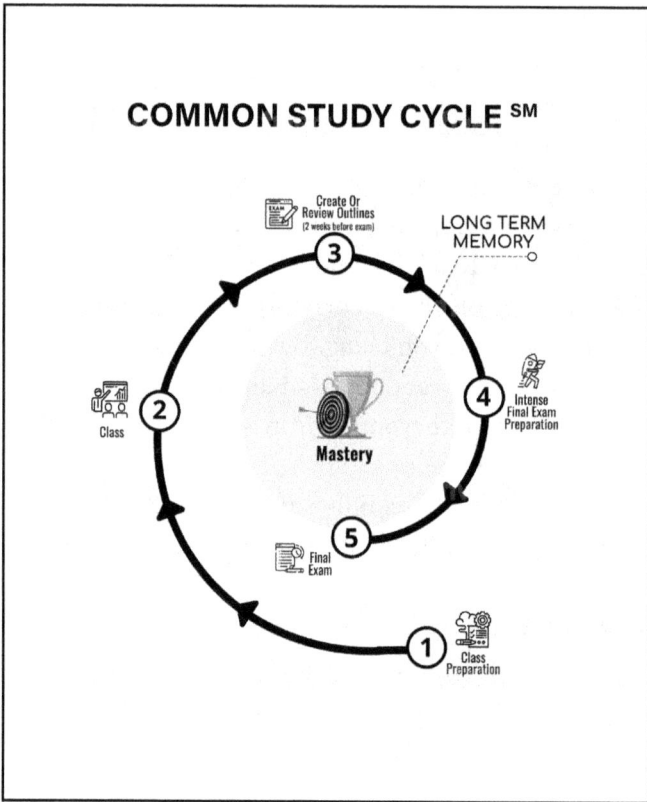

grades and passing the bar exam, with some students with low first-year grades never passing it. After graduation, many follow the same "jam and cram" strategy they used in law school, but at this point there is too much knowledge for them to cram into short-term memory in the two months before the bar exam.

When encountering legal concepts for the first time, it is imperative to move information from working (i.e., short-term) memory to long-term memory. Otherwise, as predicted by the "forgetting curve," much of that new knowledge disappears within 48 hours. This requires reviewing material on a regular basis, but, more importantly, it requires self-testing through use of flashcards and practice questions.

This is why the *Master Study Cycle*™ is superior and is the approach that should help with succeeding in law school and on the bar exam. This method requires regular engagement with the law throughout the semes-

Forgetting Curve

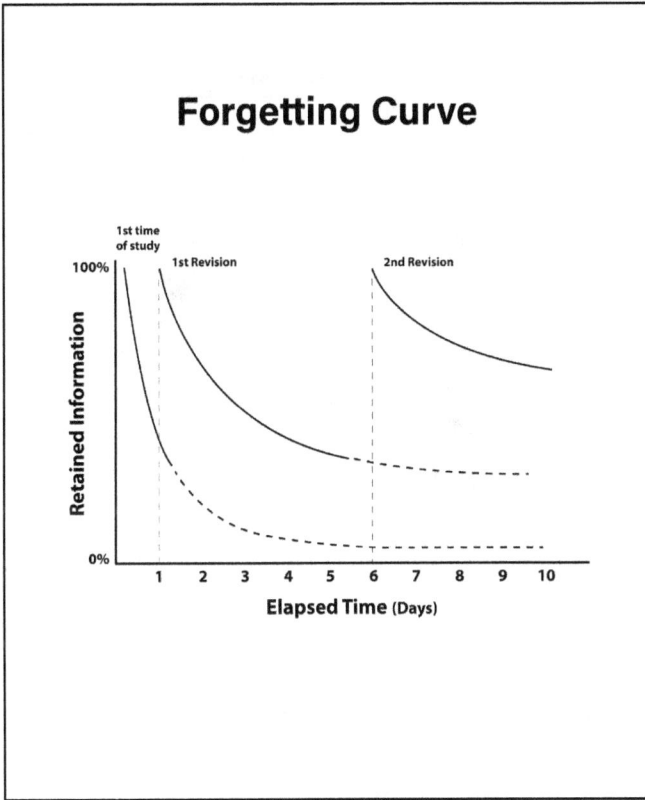

ter, not just before class and right before the final exam. To move new knowledge into long-term memory, regular review is required.

Brain Insight: Self-Regulated Learning

Self-regulated learning is a mindset students develop to control their learning environment. "Numerous empirical research has proven that greater use of self-regulated learning strategies produced better academic performance [with students learning] to manage and control their efforts on academic tasks, thus leading to persistence in learning."[2] In effect, students learn to think about their thinking—metacognition. For example, a law student writes their own study outline, a strategy to help learn the law. Next, the student compares their outline with a professionally created

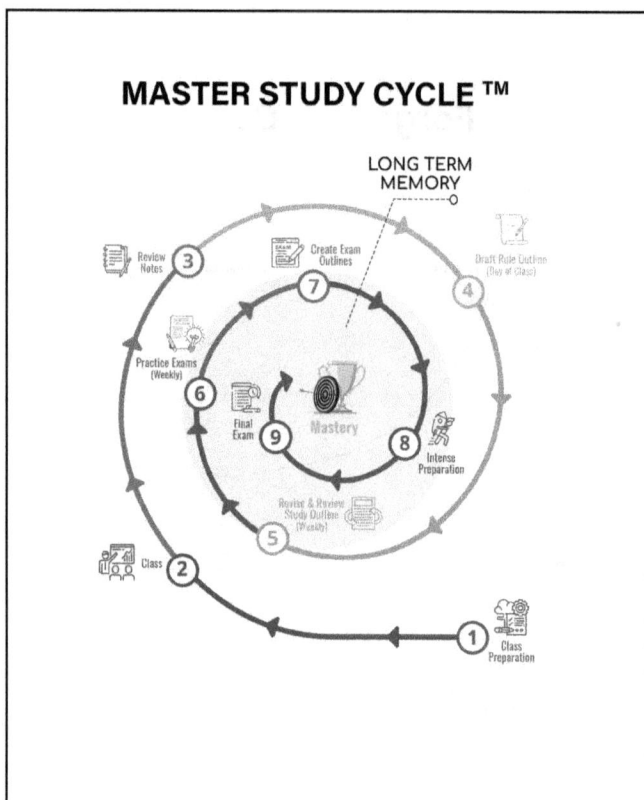

MASTER STUDY CYCLE ™

outline, looking for differences. After identifying the differences, the student thinks about why they are different and then makes changes.

STUDY AIDS: CONTEXT

Don't join an easy crowd; you won't grow. Go where the expectations and the demands to perform are high.

JIM ROHN

Appropriate use of study aids is crucial for success, while their overuse typically results in lower exam scores. A study aid is any resource that helps students prepare for a course, a class, or an exam, and they come in different forms: long, short, boring, formal, informal, interesting, visual, auditory, academic, or relatable. Study aids include resources like outlines, horn books, treatises, case briefs, audio, video, student notes from a prior year, flashcards—everything not self-created. The key is knowing when and how to use study aids for maximum learning.

Professors often advise students to never use study aids because they know many will be tempted by the allure of painless, easy knowledge. One professor, Harry Pratter, jokingly quipped to his students, "Third, and perhaps most important, this course is practical because the casebook materials and even the lectures themselves may help you understand your [study aids]."[3] But not using these resources hinders learning because students need objective material to discover their own deficiencies. Law school requires more time than most have ever spent on their studies, which leads many to find shortcuts that save time. These students gravitate to videos with titles like "Simple Hacks for Top Grades" or "How to Succeed in Law School with Minimal Effort" (not actual videos). The reality is study aids used incorrectly create a false sense of mastery, resulting in lower grades or academic dismissal. For example, someone who earns a B+ might have earned an A by using study aids the right way. The problem is study aids can create the illusion of mastery, hindering students from studying in a way that might lead to real learning. When doubts set in, and they will when you get overwhelmed with all the reading, remember this adage: "You don't know what you don't know." What I am asking you to do is suspend your disbelief and use these strategies.

The one study aid that should never or rarely be used is the professionally created case brief. Yet this is the study aid many upper-level students tell entering students to use, explaining how they could not have survived the first year without them. By the way, not every upper-level student recommends them, but because of confirmation bias, many hear only the easy advice.

A case brief is a summary of an assigned case, and it should be created on your own. Nonetheless, there are numerous professionally created case briefs, sometimes called "canned briefs," that are far superior to anything a student can produce. You are now wondering: why not use canned briefs, which are excellent, sometimes free, and recommended by seemingly successful upper-level students? Because having the perfect case brief is not the goal. If it were about possessing the perfect case brief, then it would make sense to use someone else's superior case brief. The purpose behind case briefing is to learn the law at a deep level—it's about the process, not the end product. When students read a case, they usually think they understand. In reality, they understand the case at a superficial level—enough to get by during class but not enough to get the best exam grades, let alone apply it outside class. However, when someone prepares a half-page case brief, they articulate their understanding of the case in writing. This process exposes gaps in understanding, which allows for concentrated effort on the misunderstood material. Also, as will be discussed later, the right type of case briefing can improve exam writing skills.

Most rules, including the admonition to never use canned case briefs, have a few exceptions. First, after reading a case and grappling with it for a while, it still might not make any sense. This could be for any number of reasons, including that it's 200 years old, the topic is especially challenging, or it was poorly written. Second, students get sick, impeding their concentration when reading a case. Third, there may be some other legitimate crisis keeping a student from writing their own case brief. Whatever the reason, be warned: even a good reason for using canned briefs can pave the path to dependency on using them all the time. This is similar to how some people begin using painkillers after an injury but then become addicted. Another problem is complacency, which can occur after the first few weeks of law school. Looking to lessen the workload, some tell themselves they've mastered this skill and don't need to create case briefs any longer. Bear in mind, many of the best students continue briefing their cases throughout law school because they understand it is an excellent approach to moving knowledge from working memory to long-term memory.

Let's now examine the study aids that should be used. These resources include concise horn books, treatises, outlines, audio, and video. One problem with reading cases is you generally don't have any context for the assigned material. When reading a case without some context, the brain creates a structure for it, attempting to bring order out of chaos. But the brain may create the wrong mental structure for the new concept, which some never discover. Or, the error might be discovered later during the semester, forcing the brain to pull down the wrong structure and create a new one—lots of wasted effort.

I recommend using a concise hornbook or other legal summary before beginning a new section in the casebook—any resource that explains the law the casebook is about to delve into. This helps provide context, which leads to deeper understanding. With a general understanding of the law, the cases will make more sense because of the new mental structure created by the brain. In addition, audio resources can be effective, especially when you are commuting to the law school. With all the demands on your time, an audio resource is a great way to learn new material or reinforce what you've already studied.

Finally, there are commercial outlines. Do not use someone else's outline, whether you purchased it or not, without first making your own outline. As with case briefs, outlining is about the process and the product. There are many commercially available outlines and sometimes outlines from students who aced the professor's course in a prior year. Do you know why that student earned the top grade in the class? Because they created their own outline. That student, however, will not be taking the exam for you, so recreate the process that helped them earn a top grade. Creating an outline forces engagement with the material, helping you to see how concepts are related to each other. And when something doesn't make sense, then you know to go back and review the concept. Once you create the best outline you can, compare it with a commercially created outline to expose gaps in your understanding. But only do so once you are convinced you have the perfect outline, otherwise you risk not doing the hard work yourself.

After exams, some students believe they received "good enough" grades. The "good enough" mindset is nothing more than complacency, followed by a belief they can't do better because they didn't understand the material, the professor was too hard, or the exam wasn't fair. While most students graduate law school and pass the bar exam, the best jobs and opportunities go to the top students. There is nothing wrong with lower grades if that's your best, but there are some who could have achieved more by implementing the Master Study Cycle™.

The primary reason most people who use study aids in law school never reach their full potential is because they never struggle with the law, which is essential in the learning process. Law school is hard, and struggling is normal. One professor says this about her students: "I tell them I expect them to struggle, and I tell them that if they're not struggling, they're probably not doing something right."[4] This is why study aids are potentially destructive to real learning. Imagine someone in an accident needing extensive surgery on their legs. After surgery, they initially use a wheelchair but quickly proceed to physical therapy, where they are taught to walk again. Physical therapy is slow, difficult, and painful, yet over time the person learns to walk, weaning themselves from the wheelchair. Study aids are like the wheelchair: helpful and necessary at times, but much of the time you need to walk on your own.

Student Story: Too Many Study Aids

Emma was worried she would not do well in law school, so she purchased several study aids for each course. They were written by reputable authors, but the content was duplicative and far too much to cover during the semester. Emma did not do well because she believed the quantity of material would help her succeed. The lesson from the story is purchase a few study aids, but don't purchase more than you can possibly read. If possible, look at a few sample pages from a study aid before making the purchase, and see which series seems to work for you. And when you find a series that seems to work, then purchase that series for your other courses.

Brain Insight: Cognitive Schema

Your brain is constantly making order out of chaos when it sees, hears, feels, smells, or tastes something—it immediately tries to make sense of the new stimuli. It does this by either placing it into a known schema or creating a new schema. A schema is a mental framework, like a file folder, that helps us understand the world. For example, when you see an elephant at the zoo, your brain connects it to your schema for animals, but when you see a stylized red, white, and blue elephant, your mind connects it to the schema for politics or nationalism. Maybe you are eating at an exotic restaurant, where you begin placing a new dish into categories like spicy, vegetarian, or crunchy.

When the brain encounters something new, it attempts to fit it into an existing schema, but if one doesn't yet exist, then the mind creates a new one. In law school, the brain regularly creates new schema because it doesn't have a point of reference for all the new concepts. A problem arises, however, when the brain must replace a schema created from an earlier misunderstanding. For example, when reading a case on proximate cause, the brain might connect this new legal concept to the schema dealing with things spatially close to another. Initially, this makes sense because the word proximate looks like the word proximity. And while closeness can be a factor in determining proximate cause, this new legal concept encompasses much more than spatial distance. But if the brain builds this faulty schema (i.e., connection), then it has to destroy this schema later. The end result is wasted time and mental energy building the wrong schema, destroying the old schema, and creating a new, correct schema. Not an efficient use of limited time.

When creating an outline, begin by borrowing an expert's schema to save yourself mental energy and precious time. A good place to find an expert schema for a course is the textbook's table of contents, because it provides an outline for the course. Second, the professor's list of assigned reading in the syllabus is another source, assuming they provide a categorized list; some professors provide their reading assignments only a week at a time, at the end of class. More to follow on how to create an outline.

CASEBOOKS AND CASES

You come in here with a skull full of mush... and you leave thinking like a lawyer.

PROFESSOR KINGSFIELD[5]

Almost every course uses casebooks—textbooks that are each about a thousand pages long—comprised almost exclusively of edited judicial opinions called cases. The genesis for a case begins when one person, called a plaintiff, files a lawsuit against another person, called a defendant. When talking about them together, they are called litigants, or the parties. When one or more of the litigants are unhappy with any of the trial court's legal rulings, they can appeal the legal aspects of the decision to a higher court, called an appellate court. Depending on the jurisdiction and subject matter in the case, there may two or more appellate courts. The appellate court publishes its decision, resulting in the judicial opinions used in law school casebooks. The opinions are sometimes over a hundred pages long, often discussing a multitude of issues not pertinent to the narrow issue the professor wants to cover in class. This is why the casebook author redacts the opinions to something more manageable and pedagogically sound for the topic being taught.

Along with cases, the textbook usually includes explanatory material, questions, statutes, or short essays. The judicial cases were written anywhere from a few years ago to three hundred years ago, so, in addition to learning the law, you occasionally need to read stylized forms of English not used today. Unlike other disciplines, where learning all the content in a textbook is necessary for doing well in the course, cases are used primarily by professors to facilitate classroom discussion—less than 10% of the material in a casebook appears on the exam. By understanding the purpose behind reading cases, you can adjust how to prepare for class. By way of illustration, imagine a course you take before law school, like psychology, history, or biology. A history course reading might have focused on the Protestant Reformation, with facts on the sale of indulgences, the life of Martin Luther, and the economic factors in late medieval Germany. Because the professor could use any of those facts on an exam, the study methodology focused on learning all the facts. Not so in law school.

There are three primary objectives in reading cases: classroom discussion, exam preparation, and legal reasoning development. Of the three, classroom discussion is the least important. While preparing for class is important, preparation must be understood in its broader context: classroom discussion is an indirect means in preparing students for exams. Given the importance of law school exams, it is best to remain focused on completing the *Master Study Cycle*™ tasks. In an ideal world, students attend class fully prepared to engage their professors in intellectual, profound, and meaningful discussion. But some days the professors will seem to have conspired to assign more reading than even a person with photographic memory could get to by just turning pages. Then there are colds, flat tires, sick pets, or other personal emergencies. A week rarely goes by when I don't receive an email from a student—including top performers—providing me with a reason for their lack of classroom preparation on a particular day. That's life, so don't get anxious. The key is to place classroom discussion in context and not view it in isolation from everything else that must get done each day.

To be clear, I am not suggesting students not prepare for class. By way of illustration, Dakota has eight hours a day of non-classroom time to study. Assuming she spends all eight hours reading her cases several times, reviewing them, and taking copious notes, that gets her a 100% on a hypothetical classroom preparation scale. With that 100%, she fully engages in the classroom discussion, at least on the days she is called on. But did she really need 100? Would 90 have been enough? Maybe 70, or even 50? The point is to follow a balanced studying approach, which is likely to result in long-term learning and exam success.

There is one caveat to reading cases and preparing for class. Some professors want exceptional classroom discussion, so they assign students to discuss the assigned material for a specific day—the term for this is being "on call." For example, you may find out on the first day of class that you will be on call for the class session on September 10. Or the professor might call on students in order, by row or alphabetically. My Contracts professor used this approach, starting at the top row of the room and working his way down to the front of the class over the course of the semester—given his pace, everyone knew, within a day or two, when they would be on call. When you are on call, plan to spend more time than normal preparing for that class session. Overprepare on the day you know you are on call.

The second reason for reading cases is to prepare for exams. Specifically, each case has a rule that must be placed into the outline created for each course. In Appendix 1 are several cases from a law school casebook. Briefly skim these cases, though do not look at the case briefs in Appendix 2—we will examine case briefing in the next chapter. The rule from each case is usually one sentence but might require more sentences for complex cases, cases with several exceptions, or cases with multiple factors. After capturing the rule in the case brief and verifying during class that the rule was written down correctly, the rest of the case is unimportant after the classroom discussion is over. If the professor states the rule in class, compare it with the rule in your notes and make any corrections. Unfortunately, there are days when the professor won't discuss a case or state the rule from the case, which is when a study aid can confirm that the rule in your notes is correct.

The most important reason for reading cases is legal reasoning development. A case is a judge's thought process, written down so anyone can peer into the judge's mind. This allows you to see what is important to a lawyer, and how their thought process moves from A to B to C. Developing a legal thought process doesn't occur overnight, but by reading case after case the brain learns to "think like a lawyer."

Now that you understand the purpose behind reading cases, you should begin to grasp that reading skills that worked for you in the past won't be too effective in law school. Before law school, most reading and study habits were inefficient because there was the luxury of time—plenty of time to read and study and time left over to watch a movie, play a video game, exercise, and hang out with friends. Also, reading was more attuned to learning facts, such as learning Sigmund Freud was the founder of psychoanalysis, all living thing are made up of at least one cell, or Claude Monet was part of the impressionist art movement.

It is now time to practice a law school skill by going to Appendix 1 and carefully reading *Garratt v. Dailey*. Imagine I'm your professor, asking you questions in class. Spend a few minutes writing down the answers to these questions: How old was Brian Dailey? Which court decided the case? Why did Brian move the chair? Why is Ruth Garratt suing Brian? Can a child be held liable for battery? In addition to the fall, what else would the plaintiff need to establish to show the defendant had the intent to commit a battery? Answering these and other questions might take thirty minutes of class time, and the only part of the discussion that will appear on an exam is the answer to the last question (i.e., the legal rule in the case): intent can occur when the defendant desires a result or knows to a substantial certainty the result will occur.

How to Read a Case

Read each case twice if possible. On the first read, go through the case quickly, not deeply, reading it like a light novel. The goal in the first reading is to get context for the more careful critical reading that follows. Context is important because, and this sounds obvious, you don't know what the case is about when you read it the first time. To illustrate, a discussion of the facts in a case might begin with the interaction between Todd and Lincoln. The mind, at least subconsciously, immediately goes to work trying to make sense of the case. It wonders whether Todd is the plaintiff, whether Lincoln was injured, whether either of them is the reason this case is in the book, what the legal issue is, and so on. By reading the case quickly, the mind has prepared itself for the second reading.

Read the case a second time, but this time more carefully and critically, underlining key concepts and placing important concepts into your notes. Generally, don't read a case more than twice. Also, when reading cases, don't spend time trying to master every facet of the case—there's not enough time for that, and it's not important for exam purposes. Many students think complete comprehension is essential because that's how they prepared for class in the past. Also, students worry about the possibility that the professor will call on them during class to answer a question. Suppose the professor does in fact call on you and you make mistakes. Ask yourself: what is the consequence for providing an acceptable answer versus a superb answer? The reality is there is no meaningful consequence. However, students generally fear any possible embarrassment from looking unprepared or foolish in the eyes of their peers. Assume there is some huge blunder, resulting in the class laughing out loud—it is forgotten almost immediately because everyone is more worried about themselves than they are of you. The goal is to do well on the exam by reading, studying, and reviewing. If that results in a little bit of classroom embarrassment, the momentary discomfort is well worth the prize of earning better grades and learning the law at a deep level.

Finally, there are some assigned cases with dissenting and plurality opinions. They are not binding law but instead provide insight into a judge's rationale for not joining the majority opinion—a dissenting opinion expresses disagreement with the majority's outcome, while a plurality opinion agrees with the outcome but not the majority's rationale. Very few dissenting or plurality opinions ever make it into casebooks because they are unimportant, from a pedagogical perspective. Likewise, opinion footnotes are rarely published in casebooks. But when these opinions and footnotes do appear, don't skip over them, as they are likely important. From a preparation perspective, it is unlikely the professor will let the class know in advance which ones will be discussed in class. The professor may review all of them, skip some, or ignore all of them. For some cases, the dissent is the only reason the case is included in the reading. In Appendix 1 you will find *Palsgraf v. Long Island Railroad*, a case read by almost every first-year law student. It is a relatively lengthy case, including an equally long dissent your professor will likely discuss in your torts class.

When to Read a Case

Ideally, prepare for class no earlier than 24 hours before it is scheduled. Some students read all their assigned materials for an entire week on the Saturday and Sunday before classes. While admirable, this approach is threatened by the problem of the forgetting curve, where most of what we first learn is forgotten within 48 hours. The weekends should generally be reserved for review of the prior week's work, exam preparation, and Monday's reading. Don't read too far ahead, as that is rarely an effective study method.

Second Best: Read Cases Once

There are a couple of shortcuts to reading cases twice. First, consider *skimming* the case once before completing the deep reading—understanding the context is important. Alternatively, skip the first read or skim, and instead read the case carefully as mentioned earlier. It's important to understand that life and law are full of compromises that are rarely ideal—how long to study, how long to prepare for trial, or whether to settle a case. The one shortcut you should not take is avoiding reading the case, relying instead on a canned case brief.

Professor Expectations

Professors expect students to be fully prepared to discuss the assigned material. This means a good recollection of the case facts, including those not necessarily relevant to the court's ultimate holding in the case. Expect professors to ask about unusual terms or Latin phrases in the case. While a search engine may provide most definitions, the leading source for legal terms is the most current edition of Black's Law Dictionary. Look up all unfamiliar terms, which will become familiar over time. Also, professors will ask hypothetical questions that build from the law and facts from a case. The challenge is finding enough time to prepare for each class, which is sometimes outside of your control. Imagine three classes on Tuesday, with one professor assigning 15 pages, another professor 25 pages, and a third 40 pages. With that much reading, reviewing the current day's material and case briefing might be impossible. Yet on Tuesday, each professor will expect a high level of performance from each student.

The problem isn't you; it's that few professors talk to their colleagues to coordinate daily reading assignments.

Brain Insight: Highlighting

Highlighting course material is "not significantly related to GPA."[6] Yet when observing student casebooks, I often see highlighting in almost every color of the rainbow. Unfortunately, "many students believe that these strategies are beneficial when in fact they will not always boost learning."[7] That being said, using highlighters for the purpose of remaining engaged in the reading is beneficial. But in that case, using a pen is as useful as 15 different-colored highlighters.

CASE BRIEFING

I knew that if I failed I wouldn't regret that, but I knew the one thing I might regret is not trying.

JEFF BEZOS

Case briefing is an important aspect to law school success but is rejected by most because of all the demands placed on their time. One study indicates the typical college student spends 14 hours a week studying.[8] Compared to the 50 to 60 hours needed to do well in law school, it is understandable why many dump case briefing—but this is a mistake. During law school orientation students are taught how to case brief and told to include most of the following in the case brief: case name, judge, citation, facts, procedural history, issue, holding, rule, reasoning, disposition, and notes. In an ideal, imaginary world, where students are assigned only one case per class, there would be enough time to fully complete this style of case brief. But because the real world is demanding, I recommend the FIRAC case briefing method.

The FIRAC case briefing method is designed to prepare you for class, help you remain engaged during class, and give you practice for developing essay exam writing skills. FIRAC stands for facts, issue, rule, analysis, and conclusion, or "Facts and IRAC." The IRAC exam writing method, which is discussed in Part II of the book, is the most common method for writing law school essay exams. It is also the most difficult skill students must master during their first semester if they are to succeed in law school.

Case briefing is about the process of learning the law and not about the end product. If case briefing were about the perfect brief, it would be better to purchase a professionally created brief. One of my former colleagues writes briefs for a well-known legal publisher. He graduated from a top law school, is intelligent, and writes outstanding case briefs—the perfect case briefs. But the act of creating a case brief is about learning to think critically about the law, which is also the skill needed to succeed on a law school exam. In other words, there is a correlation between case briefing and exam writing—completing one prepares you for the other. Using canned briefs is like purchasing an exercise bike and expecting to burn calories because you understand how the bike works but never use it.

When you are writing a law school exam, the IRAC exam writing method should be used or, to be more precise, the Nested IRAC exam writing method discussed in Part II. The more you practice using the IRAC exam writing method, the more likely you will see improvement on essay exams. By using FIRAC for case briefing, you not only learn the law better by engaging with the assigned material, but you also practice IRAC skills several times a day. In effect, this is a two-for-the-price-of-one method to learning.

FACTS. The facts section is needed in a case brief for only one reason: to help students remember what the case is about during the fast-paced classroom discussion. When the professor begins discussing a case, a student can, with a quick glance at the facts section, quickly recall what the case is about. In other words, the facts section is designed to activate the part of the brain where everything about the case is stored. An abundance of facts is not necessary in this section—just enough to refresh the memory. Let's work through *Garratt v. Dailey* (Appendix 1), beginning with the facts. One possibility is to write, "Five-year-old boy moved chair from where it was normally kept, resulting in Garratt falling when she tried to sit down." Don't forget that these facts are for you and no one else. Maybe all someone needs in this section is something like, "Kid moves chair, woman falls on floor." These facts don't have to be well written or follow the rules of grammar because they aren't graded, and no one else will ever read them.

ISSUE. The issue statement is the next part of the case brief. One or two sentences, written in the form of a question, provides the legal reason behind the court's decision. In other words, why is this case in the textbook? When creating an issue statement, place the plaintiff and defendant's names in the statement, along with the legal issue and the most relevant fact. It is important to be as specific as possible, capturing the narrowest legal reason the case is in the textbook. Here is one possible issue statement for the *Garratt* opinion: "Whether plaintiff can recover damages from defendant." Think about this for a minute and ask, "Is this an accurate issue statement?" Yes, it is an accurate issue statement. But it is so broad that it could be used as an issue statement for just about any torts case. Here is another statement: "Whether Garratt can sue Dailey for battery." This one is better than the first because it names both parties and the relevant tort. But it still fails to get to the narrowest legal issue in the case. One more statement: "Whether Dailey had the intent to commit a battery by moving the chair Garratt was going to sit on." Now we have an issue statement that identifies both plaintiff and defendant, the tort, the relevant element from the tort (i.e., intent), and one legally relevant fact. This statement captures the legal issue before the court and is also the kind of issue statement needed on a law school exam. (More on exams in Part II.)

RULE. The rule section provides the law that best addresses the issue identified in the prior section. Cases generally discuss many laws related to the primary issue, laws from other jurisdictions, laws from other legal areas the court found useful by way of analogy, or laws rejected by the court. The *Garratt* court provided the following rule:

> *A battery is the intentional infliction of a harmful bodily contact upon another. In order that an act may be done with the intention of bringing about a harmful or offensive contact or an apprehension thereof to a particular person, either the other or a third person, the act must be done for the purpose of causing the contact or apprehension or with knowledge on the part of the actor that such contact or apprehension is substantially certain to be produced.*

The court's definition for battery is exceptionally detailed. Now ask whether the entire rule is necessary to deal with the narrow issue in the case. For example, part of the rule mentions "either the other person or a third person." Is that necessary? What about "causing the contact or apprehension?" Go back to the case and find the narrow legal issue the court struggled with. In the final two paragraphs the court finally addresses the legal issue concerning Brian Dailey's conduct: did Brian have the necessary intent to commit a battery? But notice the court doesn't provide a clear rule statement in the final two paragraphs. Instead, the court discusses the need for the plaintiff to prove Brian "knew with substantial certainty that the plaintiff would attempt to sit down." It is up to you to create a rule statement from the court's opinion, which won't be perfect. Here is a good rule statement for *Garratt v. Dailey*: "The intent to commit a battery is present when the defendant knew to a substantial certainty that the contact would occur."

After seeing this rule statement, a student might wonder at how this rule could have been discovered by only reading the case. This would have been extremely difficult, though some might have gotten close. This is why class attendance is important, along with reviewing professional study aids to find the best rule statement for each case. After each class, review the rule in your case brief and make sure to replace it with your best understanding of the rule. This is the only portion of the case brief that needs correction after class because the rule is the only part of the case needed in preparing for exams. And as I will discuss later, the correct rule is placed into an outline created for each course.

APPLICATION. The application section, also called analysis, is where to place the reasons supporting the court's conclusion. A proper application takes a few relevant facts from the case and interweaves it with the law. From an exam preparation perspective, this is extremely important because this is the most challenging skill law students must master before exam time—practice is what helps students begin to think like a lawyer.

The first step in the application section is to recognize the most relevant facts from the case, which presupposes the correct issue was identified, along with the correct rule statement—the application section builds on the prior two sections of the case brief. A common mistake is providing too many facts, many of which are not relevant. Unfortunately, the only way to master this skill is through trial and error, with your professor hopefully helping along the way during classroom discussion. When reading a case, look for facts connected to the issue and rule. Also, though the conclusion is last, know what the court concluded before beginning this section, so the application naturally flows into the conclusion. It might help to write the conclusion before starting the application section.

Let's examine some facts to see whether they are relevant. In the first sentence we discover Brian was five years old when he visited the plaintiff on July 16, 1951. Do any of these facts help in dealing with the issue of whether Brian knew to a substantial certainty moving the chair would result in Garratt falling down? No, these facts are not relevant to answering the question. What about the fact the lawn chair was in the backyard and was made of wood and canvas? This is getting closer to the legal issue but doesn't directly address the question of whether Brian had the requisite intent to commit a battery. What about the fact he moved the chair a few feet so he could sit in the chair and when he saw her about to sit in the spot where the chair was located, he tried to move the chair back? Now, at last, we have the most relevant facts from the case, but this is only the first step in completing the application section.

The second step in creating a good application section is to connect the relevant facts to the rule statement. The most common mistake at this point is merely restating the relevant facts but then failing to explain why the facts are relevant. Professional legal writing, which is one of the outcomes in legal education, should leave very little to the imagination. When a student provides the relevant facts without an explanation as to why those facts are relevant, what they are doing is expecting the reader to determine relevancy on their own. In other words, do we want the reader to play the role of Sherlock Holmes, using their powers of observation and then deducing the correct answer by implication? No. With the *Garratt v. Dailey* case brief, imagine writing these facts:

> *Brian was in Ruth Garratt's backyard when he moved a lawn chair a few feet and then sat in the chair. When he saw Ruth Garratt about to sit in the spot where the chair had been located, he tried to move it back. But he could not get it back in time to prevent her from falling.*

Now ask, do these facts explicitly answer the question of whether Brain knew to a substantial certainty Ruth was going to fall down? They imply that but only because you've read the case. Imagine someone who never read the case was shown your case brief. Would this person have any idea these facts proved Brian didn't have the intent to cause Ruth Garratt to fall? No, they wouldn't. In legal writing, pretend the reader is someone who is unfamiliar with the law and facts. This means explicitly telling the reader why facts are relevant and not leaving it to their imagination—more on the reasons for this in Part II under exams. Let's now look at this revision:

> *Brian was in Ruth Garratt's backyard when he moved a lawn chair a few feet and then sat in the chair. When he saw Ruth Garratt about to sit in the spot where the chair had been located, he tried to move it back. But he could not get it back in time to prevent her from falling. When Brian initially moved the chair, he did not know Ruth Garratt would go back to the spot where the chair had been and then try to sit down there even though the chair had been moved.*

Someone reading this revised application section will have a much better understanding of what is being communicated.

CONCLUSION. The final section is the conclusion, which should naturally follow from the application section. The conclusion is the answer to the legal issue and not the procedural disposition of the case. For example, many students will write something like this: "The case should be dismissed in favor of Brian but is instead remanded to clarify the question of Brian's knowledge." While this does answer the procedural question of who won and the next steps in the litigation, it fails to answer the legal question of whether Brian had the knowledge to a substantial certainty Ruth Garratt would fall down. Here is a better conclusion for the case brief: "Brian did not have the intent to commit a battery because he did not know to a substantial certainty his act would result in Ruth Garratt falling down."

Here are a few more tips for case briefing. One, keep them short—they are called briefs, not longs. Generally, about half a page is adequate for most cases. Two, don't rely on someone else's briefs—create them on your own. Three, the only correction needed on a case brief after class is to the rule statement because that is the only part of the case brief used in preparing for the exam. Four, don't spend a lot of time on case briefing. Read the case twice, prepare the case brief, and then move on. What is needed is a working knowledge of the case, not completely mastery. If it is an older case, then one might need to read it a third time because of the archaic language. But as a rule of thumb, don't read a case more than twice.

When first developing this skill, plan on spending lots of time writing them, with a focus on accuracy and not speed. As with most difficult tasks in life, mastery takes time and effort. The reason most people give up on case briefing is because they don't see immediate results. Imagine someone who is not in physical shape, deciding to run in a 5K race. As they begin training, for the first weeks they might get out of breath walking around the block a few times. This is where delayed gratification begins, focusing on the end result and not where you are today. Always be mindful that the FIRAC case briefing method is designed primarily to help engage with the law at a deeper level and to develop essay exam writing skills. Don't quit.

The final two considerations are dissents and plurality opinions. As mentioned earlier, read these portions of the case because they are usually important. At the end of the conclusion section write a few sentences on the reason the dissent or plurality opinion was included in the casebook.

Second Best: Book Briefing

Book briefing is a less-than-perfect substitute for case briefing. There will be days when there isn't time to brief some, let alone all of the cases. This is especially true at the beginning of law school, when you are learning this skill. Do what you can and don't skip too many days, otherwise you will get into the habit of not doing any case briefs. Book briefing is a short-cut that identifies the F, I, R, A, and C components by making notations directly into the casebook. Place an *"F"* next to the relevant facts. Then when you spot the issue, write an *"I"* next to it, then do the same thing for R, A, and C. Many students who follow this approach decide to use different-colored highlighters for each FIRAC component.

Note: This method is for emergency purposes only! Highlighting in books is good while reading, to identify what to write down in notes. But is terrible for actually finding and then putting the law, reasoning, facts, and inferences into your own words. Book briefing, if done correctly, should be more than color-coded highlights; it should also include writing your notes in the margin of the book or, if using an e-book, placing electronic notes into the text.

The problem with this approach is many fail to grapple with the case. I've observed used casebooks where half or more of the case is highlighted with different colors. That is not case briefing but the *illusion* of case briefing. Remember there is an exam coming, and those who prepared well are more likely to receive higher grades over those who didn't. At the end of the first semester you will have a much better idea of what worked and what didn't work, so work hard from the start and avoid the shortcuts as much as possible.

Exercises

You will find a few additional cases in Appendix 1, with the case briefs in Appendix 2. Read the cases carefully, prepare the case briefs, and then look at the model answer case briefs. If you aren't happy with your case brief, try it again a few days later and then discern whether you produced a better case brief. For now, focus on accuracy rather than speed. Once you master this skill, you will complete them faster.

Student Story: Struggling to Thriving

Rosa struggled getting into law school. Though I was not her professor, she came by to talk after a disappointing first semester—she was going to be dismissed from law school if there wasn't significant improvement in her grades. She was intelligent and highly motivated to succeed but was missing a few skills necessary for law school success. I

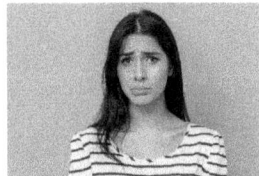

appreciated her skills deficit because I had attended academically weaker public schools until I was 14—not everyone attends the best secondary schools.

I offered to help her develop the skills she needed to get through her first year. The first short writing assignment Rosa completed was weak, and I was worried because finals were approaching in four months. I provided her with feedback and asked her to rewrite the assignment. In addition to meeting with me, she reached out to other faculty, learning from each of us. We met again a week later, but she made little improvement as she struggled to master the IRAC method. I provided more feedback and again told her to rewrite the same assignment.

During our second meeting she shared the personal sacrifices she was making to succeed: sleeping less, staying at the law school longer, exercising and attending church less frequently, and dropping out of a study group that wasn't helping her. These may not be the same choices you might make, but they were what she had decided were needed to help her achieve her goals.

At our third meeting, I was pleasantly surprised by her revised assignment. It was well written, taking into account all of the prior feedback. Rosa later told me that in one class, the professor had asked to use her answer as a model answer for the other students in the class. This was a wonderful turnaround, in large part because Rosa was willing to delay her immediate gratification in things she wanted, like more sleep, and spent that time improving her study and exam skills. When second semester grades were released, Rosa's grades improved significantly, allowing her to continue her studies.

Brain Insight: Delayed Gratification

Successful people learn to delay their gratification, which occurs when you resist a small temptation today for something more important you want tomorrow. Should you eat pizza every day or only once every few weeks to avoid gaining weight? Spend hours on social media or exercise? The idea of delayed gratification applies not only to physical health but also to academic success. To illustrate this concept, imagine returning home after a busy day at school. The options are reading for another few hours or watching a favorite TV show. Intellectually, the right choice is reading, yet many choose to not delay their immediate desire to watch some TV. And because the cost of doing so is delayed by months or years, it is not felt immediately. In Parts II and III are several techniques to help develop delayed gratification skills.

HOW TO STUDY

Law school is a test—not a test of strength, creativity, or intelligence—but one of endurance. A law student's greatest nemesis is not mastering legal concepts, but enduring the hours of solitude, which endless studying requires.

KILROY J. OLDSTER

There isn't enough time in the day to complete everything that needs to get done, at least if perfection is the goal. In large part this is because of all the required reading. Managing the assigned reading requires becoming more efficient at reading legal material. A common reading strategy before law school involved reading the same material several times, and after the second, third, or fourth reading the material was generally understood. Then, a week before final exams, students reviewed the course material again, which placed the knowledge into working memory but not long-term memory. The course content was retained in short-term memory just long enough to do well on an exam. This strategy will not work in law school. Law students do not have the time to use that old approach and also complete the Master Study Plan™. Also, the old approach was never an effective learning method. While it may have worked to get top grades in college, that was only because students had the luxury of wasting time on an inefficient learning method.

Becoming a stronger student requires a few changes to study methods, thereby maximizing the brain's learning capacity. Alluded to earlier, some will choose to spend more hours studying, believing success is measured by how long one studies. The amount of time spent studying is important, but more critical is learning to study differently. The brain craves variety, so one way of keeping the brain from getting bored is to give it what it wants. First, avoid spending more than one hour on any one subject. Each day, divide the reading into one-hour segments. Read torts for an hour, then shift to contracts, then to civil procedure, and then back to torts. Studies indicate humans learn material at a deeper level by changing topics regularly. When beginning this new study routine, it will feel uncomfortable. This is because most students are used to starting one subject and not stopping until they are completely done with that subject. The natural reaction to starting something new, difficult, and uncomfortable is returning to the familiar. For example, many people today never take a formal typing class, where they learn to use all ten fingers on the keyboard. When someone decides to begin typing with all ten fingers, they may quit because it is awkward and return to using only a few fingers. Intuitively one understands using all fingers is faster and less tiring, yet many don't persevere to learn the better skill—short-term pain for long-term gain.

A second approach to improved learning is taking frequent breaks when studying. This is because the brain has an optimal learning level, and regular breaks keep the brain functioning near that level. A common experience is reading for an hour and suddenly discovering you have no idea what you've been reading—wasted time. Imagine the brain as a completely dry sponge when study time begins. The act of studying slowly adds water to the sponge until it is completely full. At that point, studying is no longer possible because the sponge is at capacity. Just like a soaking-wet sponge that must be squeezed for it to continue absorbing water, it takes the brain time to recover from continuous mental use. While someone can continue to read, the brain no longer is absorbing new material. However, by taking short, regular breaks, the brain regains some of its ability to continue studying effectively. This same mechanism occurs at night when we allow our brains to rest. The Pomodoro Technique, discussed later in the Time Management chapter, is used by millions for implementing frequent study breaks into a schedule—it is the technique I am using as I write these words.

Sooner or later everyone hits a roadblock when encountering difficult material. One reaction is giving up immediately and going to see the professor—this is a mistake. When struggling with the reading, place a small "S" in the margin of that paragraph, where the "S" represents the word *struggling*. Often, within a few more paragraphs the problem will clear itself. At other times, there may be a page or two full of marks. Learning law at a deep level requires struggling, using the brain to reach an answer by itself. But many students give up when they get frustrated because they want the answer right away. Easy answers rarely result in meaningful learning.

After reaching the point of wanting to give up, use the 15-minute solution developed by former Cornell University president Dale Corson. Get paper and a timer. Set the timer for 15 minutes, go back to each "S" in the margin, and begin taking notes. Write down exactly what doesn't make sense in the reading. What is causing the confusion? Explain it in writing, not stopping until the answer comes to you or the timer goes off. Some wonder why they should spend any more time on a concept that has eluded them up to this point. There are two reasons. First, starting this process often relaxes the mind just enough to solve the problem on its own because there is an end in sight. Second, the writing process is one of purposeful self-reflection, which allows the mind to think differently about the reading. But sometimes the problem does not resolve itself within 15 minutes. This is the point at which you would seek help from the professor. Take the 15 minutes' worth of notes to the professor, which allows you to explain where the confusion lies. Students who struggle through difficult material will often master the law, compared to those who are satisfied with a superficial understanding. The best students work hard at exercising their intellect.

Student Story: Working Hard and Not Quitting

Richard moved across country to attend law school in North Carolina. He didn't have a lot of money, so lunch normally consisted of a candy bar. Richard was serious about his studies, spending most of his free time in the library. One day, Richard saw a professor in the library and confided in him he was thinking about quitting. The professor told him not to quit because he saw Richard all the time in the library preparing for class—the ability to sit and keep working was, according to the professor, the hallmark for success. Richard continued his legal studies and eventually became the 37TH President of the United States.

STUDY NOTES

*When I got to law school, I didn't do very well.... In fact,
graduated in the part of my law school class that made the top
90% possible.*

Daniel H. Pink

To succeed in law school, consider creating three sets of notes: comprehensive, study outline, and notes at a glance.

The *comprehensive* set includes everything written down during the semester, including case briefs, class notes, and post-class notes. This comprehensive set is far too large to work with in preparing for an exam and needs to be condensed into a shorter study outline.

The *study outline*, also called a rule outline, is comprised of the legal rules covered in a course. From the case briefs, copy the rules but not the facts, issues, application, or conclusion. The study outline will not include in-class hypotheticals, policy statements, or other extraneous materials from class—only the rules that will appear on the exam. If the professor mentions that a law won't be on the exam, then do not place it into the study outline. For many classes, the professor does not require students to provide case names on exams, so in those classes do not place them into the study outline. However, some classes—generally Constitutional Law and parts of Civil Procedure—do require case names on the exam, which therefore should be included in the study outline. Ask the professor early in the semester if they prefer case names on an exam, then prepare the study outline accordingly. Once the study outline is created, this is the primary document used in preparing for the exam.

The primary problems with self-generated study outlines are the errors and missing information, which is why commercial study aids are indispensable. Comparing your study outline with a professionally created outline or another student outline is for the sole purpose of exposing gaps in your knowledge. It is either naïve or arrogant (or both!) to believe you can create the perfect study outline on your own—even professors talk to each other to help them understand complex legal principles. On the other extreme is the person who doesn't create their own outline and relies solely on a commercial outline. As mentioned earlier with case briefing, the purpose behind creating a study outline is not the end product but the process. First, the brain makes stronger connections to legal content each time an interaction occurs. The very act of taking a rule from a case brief and then placing it into the rule outline strengthens the neural connection to the rule, making it easier to use the rule on the exam. Second, each time an interaction occurs with a different sense, it strengthens the neural connections to the law. Reading is a visual sense connection, and typing is a tactile sense connection.

Commercial outlines are useful when used wisely. Before using this essential comparison tool, create the best study outline possible with your notes and course material. Pretend you don't have a commercial study outline, and struggle through creating it on your own. What some students do is create a weak outline, knowing a commercial outline is waiting for them, but this creates only the illusion of learning and not actual deep learning. Once you believe you have the *perfect* study outline, then, and only then, compare your self-created study outline with a commercial product. When you see mistakes, it should sting a bit because you created the "perfect outline." Next, when you see a difference between the two documents, stop and reflect on the difference. There may be a gap in your knowledge, a difference in how the law is explained in the commercial product, or coverage on a law not discussed by the professor.

The third document is the *notes at a glance*, which is needed to help unlock the study outline on exam day. The notes at a glance, or short outline, should be about one page long. The plan is to synthesize the most important rules from the course, which you commit to memory. But why memorize anything? On exam day it is natural to get anxious, which can lead to the temporary inability to access information in the brain. When this happens, your memorization outline will help open the locked part of the brain. Suppose on exam day a question involves whether a contract was formed or not. Suddenly the brain locks up. The notes at a glance, which you memorized, state every contract requires an offer, acceptance, and consideration. And with a memorized key, the rest of the knowledge on contract formation should come flooding back into your working memory.

You may be wondering, "Why memorize only one page and not the entire study outline?" The answer is most people are not taught to memorize vast amounts of information, but almost anyone can memorize about one page. I once had two students from Korea take a closed-book exam from their home, with an honor code prohibiting them from looking at their notes during the exam. Their answers quoted vast amounts of law directly from the textbook, and I was convinced they had cheated. I later learned they memorized their textbooks because in Korea they were trained from a young age to memorize information. But in most countries, a page to a page and a half is about the most we can hope to memorize.

One final note on the "three sets of notes" method on open-book exams: use the method! Many students who take open-book exams fail to adequately prepare for their exams, believing they have time to review their notes and commercial study aids during the exam. That doesn't work. Having attended a law school where almost every exam was open book, one develops a false sense of security by having every possible resource available during a timed exam. There simply isn't time during an exam to review notes and open books often; most of the exam time is needed to read the question, develop a short exam outline, and then apply the law to the facts. Open-book exams are a trap for the unwary.

Student Story: Twenty-Hour Days

 Victoria was in her first year of law school in New York when she reached out to me. She had received her first-semester grades and was upset because they were much lower than she expected. She had worked hard, received verbal affirmation from her professors, completed her reading each night, and was always prepared to answer questions in class. As she shared her story, she mentioned that to keep up with the reading, she had scheduled every minute in her day, including only four hours of sleep a night. Without any

hesitation, I immediately said, "Victoria, you can't keep doing this or you are going to collapse." In case you are wondering, Victoria was an exceptionally bright person, and her weak exam scores were not based on intelligence or work ethic. If discipline, hard work, determination, grit, and self-denial were all one needed for success, Victoria would have earned top grades. But that wasn't enough. During her second semester we worked on improving her exam preparation, exam-taking skills, reading strategies, and several other skills. At the end of the second semester, she moved from below-average grades to the top of the class while also getting back to sleeping seven hours a night.

CLASSROOM DISCUSSION

We lawyers are always curious, always inquisitive, always picking up odds and ends for our patchwork minds, since there is no knowing when and where they may fit into some corner.

CHARLES DICKENS

Law professors tend to utilize the case method, also called the Socratic method, to help students develop legal reasoning skills. Classroom discussion is a dialogue between student and professor, with the professor guiding the discussion by asking questions about facts in a case, law, procedure, hypotheticals derived from a case, policy, philosophical underpinnings, or anything else that comes into the professor's mind. It is generally unscripted—the professor poses new questions depending on students' responses. In the following quote from the 1973 movie *The Paper Chase*, fictional law professor Charles Kingsfield explains the Socratic method this way:

> *The study of law is something new and unfamiliar to most of you—unlike any schooling you have ever been through before. We use the Socratic method here. I call on you, ask you a question, and you answer it. Why don't I just give you a lecture? Because through my questions you learn to teach yourselves. Through this method of questioning, answering, questioning, answering, we seek to develop in you the ability to analyze that vast complex of facts that constitute the relationships of members within a given society. Questioning and answering. At times, you may feel that you have found the correct answer. I assure you that this is a total delusion on your part. You will never find the correct, absolute, and final answer. In my classroom, there is always another question, another question to follow your answer. Yes, you're on a*

treadmill. My little questions spin the tumblers of your mind.
You're on an operating table; my little questions are the fingers
probing your brain. We do brain surgery here. You teach
yourselves the law, but I train your mind. You come in here with
a skull full of mush, and you leave thinking like a lawyer.

The professor needs students to answer questions and thus might rely on volunteers or call on students to answer their questions. Depending on the professor, students might receive advance notice as to the day they are "on call," while other professors go down the row student by student, some alphabetically, and some "cold call." In this last approach, students have no notice of when they will get called, which can lead to some anxiety. I use the cold-call approach because it requires everyone to prepare fully for each class.

Imagine the professor unexpectedly calling on you to "please recite the facts in *Garratt v. Dailey.*" You get three to five seconds to begin responding; otherwise the professor moves to someone else. Naturally, this creates some level of anxiety. Though prepared, you freeze momentarily because the amygdala—a small part in the middle of the brain—immediately sends fear responses to the rest of the body. The prefrontal cortex then goes to work, attempting to gain control so you can answer the question rationally. If you are prepared and need a moment to collect your thoughts, you might want to tell the professor something like "I am prepared to discuss the case but need a moment to refresh my memory." This will get you a few additional seconds as the professor knows you are prepared.

Let's take a closer look at the Socratic method. The method is named after Socrates, a Greek philosopher who lived in Athens in the fifth century B.C. Though Socrates never wrote anything, his student Plato captured his teachings in a series of books called the Dialogues. In the Dialogues, Socrates asks question after question of other characters, trying to get them, through the use of logic and reason, to admit the truth or falsehood of major and minor issues. His most famous dialogue is called *Phaedo*, where Socrates asks questions of his students on the immortality of the soul. It's a wonderful, short book, if you've never read any of the Dialogues.

The Socratic method is a great teaching tool because it helps keep students engaged, which is in stark contrast to the traditional lecture. Some questions are designed to elicit lower-level-thinking answers. For example, "In what year did the American Revolution begin?" A simple "1776" is all that is needed. But the Socratic method is used to engage higher-level thinking, as when the professor asks, "Why did the American colonies revolt in 1776?"

Professors use this teaching method in different ways. Approach #1 is the boot camp approach. The professor's sole purpose in asking questions is to break the student by asking question after question until the student fails. This establishes the professor's dominance and humbles the student, so the student is willing to learn. This is the approach used in military training, where the new recruit is psychologically torn down so they can be trained in the new military method. This approach isn't used much in legal education today.

Approach #2 is the accountability approach. The professor asks questions of many students during each class session, but most of the questions require little thought. The professor does this to ensure students read the material and continue to prepare for class. Failure to answer a question might result in the professor noting the lack of preparation, possibly resulting in a lower course grade. Also, the professor might ask more questions to the unprepared student in future class sessions.

Approach #3 is the thinking approach, which most closely resembles how Socrates interacted with others. During a class session, the professor asks questions of only a few students. Each student answers questions for 15 to 20 minutes as the professor tries to get the student to explain something from the assigned material. For example, the professor may ask, "Mr. Smith, why do you believe the court ruled in favor of the defendant?" The professor will also ask hypothetical questions, which requires the student to move beyond the assigned reading. "Mr. Smith, that is a correct understanding of the case. Now, let's change the facts. Assume the victim was holding a gun instead of a baseball bat. How does that change your answer?" Then there are policy questions, such as "Mr. Smith, what is the policy behind the court's decision, and what are the likely repercussions in future lower court rulings?"

It is possible to survive and thrive in a Socratic environment. First and foremost, come to class fully prepared. Read the assigned material, prepare case briefs, and read a study aid that explains the concepts to be discussed in class. Remember, this is a dialogue, so lack of preparation will lead to a general lack of engagement. Second, when the professor asks someone else a question, pretend the professor asked you the question. Then answer the question in your mind and compare your mental answer to what the other student says. Passive listening is the quickest way to boredom and lack of engagement, which defeats the main benefit of the Socratic method. Also, when other students are talking with the professor, keep in mind they might be completely wrong in their response. The professor might not correct them, instead continuing a dialogue to see where the student will go with the incorrect facts or law. Third, when called on to answer a question, look at the professor when answering the question. Often the answers are nowhere to be found in your notes or reading, so don't look for them. Stop, think, and answer. If it's taking time to formulate an answer, it is acceptable to tell the professor something like this: "I know the answer, but I need a few seconds to gather my thoughts." Fourth, if you don't understand the professor's question, ask the professor to rephrase it. Fifth, try to answer the question if you are prepared. The case method is not about giving a perfect answer. And by trying, you might get to the right answer—nothing ventured, nothing gained. A skilled professor will generally work with a struggling student to get to the right answer, assuming there is even a right answer to get to. What I tell my students is I would rather see them try and get it completely wrong than for them to never have tried at all. Classroom discussion is about learning to think like a lawyer, where we learn not only from our successes but also from our failures.

Student Story: Socratic Nightmares

Jane was called on by the professor to answer a question. After she attempted to answer the question, the professor stared at her for a moment and then walked over to the classroom light switch. He then turned off the lights and

said, "This is what I think about that answer." The class laughed, but it left Jane in tears.

At another law school, a former colleague expected everyone to be prepared for his class—if not prepared, then it was best to not attend class. He used the cold-call method, which meant no one was ever too sure when they were going to be called. To ensure students were fully prepared, he explained that anyone not prepared for the discussion would be asked to leave the room. He enforced the rule, so many students chose to listen outside the classroom door rather than risk getting caught unprepared. These stories are becoming less common, with most faculty today employing fewer fear and shame-based strategies.

Brain Insight: Fear or Rational Control

Fear is a natural reaction designed to keep you safe by accelerating breathing, increasing the heart rate, dilating pupils, and sending additional glucose to the muscles. While this is exactly what should happen when encountering a bear in the woods, this is an ineffective response when required to think rather than run or fight. For most students, hearing their name called by the professor triggers the fear response, at least momentarily. While most students are able to regain emotional control quickly, some struggle throughout their interaction with the professor.

There are several techniques for reducing the fight-or-flight response so one can think more clearly. One, take a deep breath, which signals the brain that there is no need to fear. Two, inside your mind tell yourself this is normal and you can do this. And three, focus on the question, not the professor.

CLASSROOM NOTETAKING

The young lawyer knows the rules, but the old lawyer knows the exceptions.

OLIVER WENDALL HOLMES, JR.

Taking classroom notes in law school is unlike notetaking strategies that worked well in the past. As explained earlier, very little from the classroom discussion appears on the law school exam. During class stay engaged and don't mindlessly copy everything said by classmates or the professor. In most undergraduate programs, professors spend class time primarily emphasizing the most important content from the assigned reading, requiring students to take copious notes. This makes perfect sense when an exam is focused on assessing knowledge. When taking notes, always keep the end in mind. Ask yourself, "What part of the classroom discussion will help me on the final exam?"

The vast majority of law school exams require students to apply the law to a set of facts they've never seen before exam day. With this end in mind, step number one in a classroom discussion is to identify the law the professor is going to use on an exam. It is critically important to understand the exact rule the professor uses because unlike chemistry, there is rarely only one way to articulate a rule. The first case in the textbook may state the rule one way, the next case may state it slightly differently, and a study aid may state it yet a third way. When the professor provides the class with the rule, either on the board, on the screen, or verbally, place the rule into your notes.

For the typical ninety-minute law school class session, expect to write about half a page of notes dedicated to the rules. Each case ordinarily represents one rule, with one rule normally written in a single sentence. There are other things to capture in your notes. A few professors might expect students to provide policy rationales on their exams, so write down those when they are discussed in class. At the beginning of the semester, it might be difficult to know exactly what the professor will want on the exam, but see whether the professor has posted any old exams or whether the law school keeps old exams in the library or on their website. You can also just ask the professor what they expect on the final exam.

Anytime the professor says, "This is important," write it down. This is a major clue that it is likely to appear on the exam. Next, listen for recurring themes and words the professor keeps repeating. This will help in determining the types of issues that motivate the professor, providing some insight into the kinds of questions they may ask. If the professor writes information on the board, like a numbered list or rule of law, place it in your notes. Given the fast-paced nature of class, when the professor references a rule from the textbook, jot down the reference and later place the rule into your study outline. If the class is recorded, listen to find the exact words the professor used for the rule, placing them into your study outline. Finally, consider writing down some of the hypotheticals that come up in class. While the hypothetical won't likely be identical to one discussed in class, it might be close enough to provide insight into the professor's mindset.

Now let's discuss what *not* to write down. Not everything the professor says or asks is important. In fact, most of the classroom discussion is directed at getting students to understand the facts and law from a particular case. Do not write down any clarification of the facts from a case that help you understand the case better. Unless this is a class in Constitutional law, the facts from the case are useless the moment class is over. For example, many law students read *Pennoyer v. Neff* in Civil Procedure. It is a faculty-confusing nineteenth-century case, which might tempt you to write down clarifying facts provided by the professor. Don't waste intellectual resources writing facts that are completely useless for exam purposes. Also, don't write down what other students say, unless the professor says something like "she just articulated the correct rule of law."

Student Story: Too Many Class Notes

Greyson could type fast, so he took near verbatim notes in class, capturing what the professor and students were saying. For each class session

Greyson was able to type about ten pages. He then spent time rereading those pages, following the learning script he had been taught in college. Unfortunately, he did not do well on the final exam because he did not use a more effective study method. The moral to the story is verbatim notes are not magical and will deter learning. It's like watching or listening to a class recording over and over again—not effective for long-term learning.

Brain Insight: Handwriting or Typing

A few years ago, a scientific study was conducted with Princeton and UCLA students. The researchers compared students who typed their notes on laptops with students who handwrote their class notes. Those who handwrote their class notes earned higher grades. Before explaining the scientific reason for the result, let me share a story from a court reporter. If you don't know what they do, a court reporter is the person who sits in the courtroom and types out a verbatim transcript of what is said at trial. At the end of one trial, an attorney asked the court reporter if she was shocked by what she heard from the defendant. She looked at the attorney and told him she had no idea what the defendant had said since she was thinking about what she had to do at home later that day.

This phenomena of being able to type and not listen is exactly what goes on in the classroom. People talk much faster than we can possibly handwrite, meaning those who write out their notes must summarize what they hear. In other words, people who take notes by hand process information while also taking notes. That is not true for those who type. People can type just about as fast as someone talks, which activates the part of the brain used for transcribing—a part that is not engaging with the material and instead is merely listening for accuracy. In other words, people who type their notes are not thinking about the material compared to those who are handwriting their notes.

STUDY OUTLINE
(RULE OUTLINE)

Law school is a test—not a test of strength, creativity, or intelligence—but one of endurance. A law student's greatest nemesis is not mastering legal concepts, but enduring the hours of solitude, which endless studying requires.

KILROY J. OLDSTER

The study outline, mentioned earlier under Study Notes, is the most important document created in preparation for an exam. This is where all the rules from a course are placed, often resulting in a 20 to 50 page document for each doctrinal course. The first step in creating a study outline is to find an expert's brief outline for the course, which lists the course categories in a systemized manner. Also called a skeletal outline, this is an outline created by an expert, providing structure for the rules you will place into it throughout the semester. A textbook's table of contents is a good place to find this framework as it organizes the course content. Also, some professors provide a detailed syllabus, which might serve as a skeletal outline. Once this broad structure is complete, feel free to make changes throughout the semester—it's a starting point to help guide the way. In Appendix 5 is an example taken from a popular Property casebook. Notice the headings and subheadings, underneath which you will place the rules covered in the course.

The next step is to place rules into the outline as the course progresses. The only thing placed into the outline are the rules, generally not case names or facts from the cases. The rules and exceptions to those rules should be written concisely, in words you understand but that are also legally accurate. For example, a case from 1894 might state the law as follows: "the wrong inflicted, when the defendant so did with intent, and with force that contacted the victim's person, must result in adequate compensation for the injury." Take the archaic language and write something like this: "A defendant's intentional contact with the victim will result in the defendant paying damages." A caveat on placing only rules into an outline: some professors might want students to make analogies from cases to the facts on their exams. For example, "as in *Palsgraf v. Long Island Railroad*, this plaintiff was not within the zone of foreseeable risk." For professors who want analogies, include case names and a few facts from the case into the outline.

Let's discuss common mistakes when creating the rule outline. A typical error is taking all of the class notes, rearranging them, and then placing them into an outline. That is not a study outline but, rather, rearranged notes. Next, think about the outline's size. Since the outline is the primary tool used to prepare for the final exam, it should be concise—short, accurate, and to-the-point rule statements. For example, a 15-word rule statement is better than a 22-word rule statement.

After creating the perfect outline, then, and only then, look at an outline created by someone else. Notice the differences but don't make changes immediately. Think about the differences. Ask yourself, "Why are they different?" You may find your outline is better in some places or that you missed something. When you discover errors, go back to find out why you made those errors. This reveals gaps in your knowledge and, potentially, in your understanding of the law. If you stop to reflect, you learn the law in a way that helps you earn a higher score on the exam. Those who rely solely, or heavily, on outlines created by others create the illusion they know the law. But they are failing to make the connections necessary to get high grades.

Finally, not every class requires the same type of outline or even any outline. Take, for example, a class on legal writing—a skills course, not a doctrinal course. This class doesn't teach law, but instead writing skills. Also, the course assessments revolve around writing exercises. This and some other law school courses do not require a study outline. Remain flexible and find an approach that works for the course.

Student Story: Creative Study Outlines

Jessica found she did not have the time to create a traditional outline. For years, she had placed important notes onto sticky notes, which helped her learn new material. She continued this habit in law school and eventually came up with a variation: write related concepts on the same-colored sticky notes and then place them on a large poster board. In contracts, all offer-related concepts were placed on pink sticky notes, acceptance on yellow, and consideration on light green—Jessica used more than a dozen different colors on her sticky board outline.

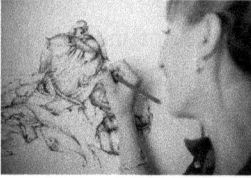

Kristi was an artist who found traditional outlining confusing—it simply wasn't how her mind organized material. Her approach was to draw, placing rules into her drawings. In Torts, Kristi drew a large tree with large roots and branches. One big root was labeled *Negligence*, with smaller roots connected to it labeled *duty, breach, causation,* and *harm*. Then those smaller roots had even smaller roots with related terms. These pen drawings were not only beautiful, but they helped Kristi learn the law.

REVIEWING

The pursuit of learning is to increase day after day.

TAO-TE CHING

Regularly reviewing study notes leads to deeper learning and better scores on an exam— learning is a marathon, not a sprint. Many students begin their exam review only when they are close to the exam, cramming the law into their minds. That is an ineffective means to learn material because the human brain needs more time to learn complex material. For example, imagine someone deciding to save time by eating their weekly 14,000 caloric requirements at one sitting—twenty pints of high-calorie ice cream should do the trick. The body cannot effectively digest this amount of food at one sitting, and within a few days the body will need more calories. It is the same way with processing new information. A slow and steady intake throughout the semester is the most effective approach to learning law.

The first step in the review process is to quickly review each day's notes, which, if done correctly, should not be much more than one page per class. Second, review the rules, make quick necessary revisions, and place them into the study outline. Don't worry about making them perfect at this point; just place them into the outline. The third, and most crucial step, is to revise and review the study outline once a week. This is when the most recently added rules are revised, and then the entire rule outline is reviewed. During the review, stop and reflect on anything that doesn't make sense, and feel free to make changes to the outline based on your better understanding of the law.

Imagine covering "duty of care," then placing this rule into the study outline. A few weeks later, a new case discusses duty of care in a different context, providing new insight into the concept. Make corrections to the study outline, using this latest understanding as a guide. A study outline is not static but should change throughout the semester as it is reviewed and revised. Each time one goes through this process, the brain makes stronger neural connections to the law, and new pathways are made connecting legal concepts together.

Brain Insight: Spaced Repetition

Practice makes perfect, but when and how we practice is critical for optimal learning. Many students learned to study using the block method, where material is studied during one block of time—cramming is a good example, where someone spends three days before an exam learning the material for one course. Spaced repetition takes advantage of the spacing effect, where the same amount of time is used but is spread out over time. This effect was first noticed in 1885, and since then numerous studies have demonstrated its superiority to the block method.[9] To illustrate, suppose a Contracts course is taught over 12 weeks and there are 50 hours available for post-class review. It is better to spend four hours a week reviewing instead of cramming those 50 hours into the two-week period before the final exam.

Student Story: Lower Performance on Last Final

This story involves an observation involving my students over time and their average class performance depending on final exam order. As a professor in the first-year curriculum, in some years my final exam is given first, in the middle, or last in the exam schedule—after a decade of teaching I noticed a pattern. In the years students took my final exam first, their answers were superb, showing a strong understanding of the material. In those same years, when my exam was first, in the days preceding the final many students came by my office and asked good questions. In contrast, when my final exam was last, very few students came by to ask questions, and overall exam performance was significantly weaker.

While there are different reasons for this, including exam fatigue, the most likely cause is heavy reliance on the cramming strategy. Whichever final exam comes first in the schedule, students spend three to five days preparing for that final. After that, they may have only a day or two between final exams. From a grading perspective, when I have the last final exam, this means less time grading because students were unable to write as much. However, the law school's mandatory grading policy ensures, on average, grades remain the same from year to year.

Understanding this dynamic provides a savvy student with a slight advantage. By using spaced repetition throughout the semester, this student's exam performance should be about the same for all their final exams. In contrast, the cramming student will see a gradual decrease in their exam performance during the final exam period. The student who uses spaced repetition can compensate for the cramming student's better performance on the first final by studying a bit longer for the first final. And then, because of the law school's mandatory grading policy, the spaced repetition student's last final exam should rank a bit higher than the cramming student's exam, earning the spaced repetition student an even higher grade on that last final exam.

PART II: EXAMS & ADVANCED SKILLS

To the man who only has a hammer, everything he encounters begins to look like a nail.

ABRAHAM MASLOW

Law school exams are not designed to measure competency but to rank students from top to bottom. The students with the highest grades generally serve on law review, in moot court, or as faculty research assistants. And after law school, grades remain important for securing jobs and judicial clerkships. Some employers, decades after graduation, request the law school transcripts of a potential employee. The goal in law school is not only to become a lawyer but also to position oneself to receive opportunities throughout life.

Few people enter law school with the exam and study skills necessary to succeed. Many believe superior study skills are achieved by working longer hours, which is partially true. I've had students come to my office after exams, confused because they did not earn high grades even though they "put in the time." Success requires understanding law school exams, which takes time—this is not a skill mastered two weeks before the final exam. Developing this new skill is arduous because law school exams, in a sense, are not traditional academic exercises. The law school exam is designed to somewhat mimic legal writing, which is radically different from the writing most encountered before law school. This means learning to write in a style acceptable to practicing lawyers. Never lose sight of the fact that legal education is not primarily concerned with the law but rather with developing higher-level thinking skills—application, analysis, and evaluation. This is because most lawyers, in a typical case, can find the law within a few minutes.

Traditionally, law school exams were only essay questions, but today more professors are using bar exam-style multiple-choice questions. Both the essays and multiple-choice questions are different from those used in undergraduate programs. A typical college essay question requires students to provide facts from the course, with students who provide the most facts earning the highest marks. Likewise, college multiple-choice questions generally test for knowledge comprehension, with only one possible correct answer. In contrast, law school multiple-choice questions might have multiple correct answers, requiring students to pick the best answer. And harder yet, sometimes all the options on a law school multiple-choice question are technically incorrect, requiring students to pick the least incorrect answer.

The examination process also varies among law schools and among professors. Exams are almost always proctored by someone other than the professor and are closed book, open book, or somewhere in between. An open-book exam generally means books and notes are allowed in the exam room, though a professor may limit which other material may be used. For example, the professor might allow the casebook but no notes, or the casebook as long as it doesn't include many handwritten student notes in the margins, or three pages of notes. Some professors choose a completely closed-book exam because it resembles the bar exam. The exams have different time limits for completing them, often based on the course's number of credits—a three-credit course has a three-hour final exam.

Many students find it unusual that law professors do not proctor their own exams. This is because law school exams are almost always anonymous, with the administration assigning blind grading numbers to place on the exam instead of names. With a blind grading process, professors don't proctor their own exams for fear they might identify a student's handwriting or recognize a phrase on their computer, thereby destroying the anonymity. Some schools even prohibit professors from going near the exam room in case they peer into the classroom and somehow identify a student's identity. Afterwards, the professor grades the exams without knowing who wrote the exam. The purpose behind this system is to encourage classroom discussion, freeing students from perceived retaliation by their professors. This system also protects professors from giving higher grades to students they believe were brighter than reflected in their exam performance. The goal is to remove as much subjectivity from the grading process as possible, protecting the professor from claims he or she lowered or raised a grade based on anything other than exam performance.

What follows next is a look at the law school exam itself, and then an exploration into exam strategies for improving exam performance. Understanding law school exams is only the first step towards mastery. Success requires a multilayered approach to learning law, developing exam tactics, and, finally, using post-exam self-reflection strategies for improvement. The key is pacing throughout the semester, not one massive cramming session days before the final exam.

One caveat: this book introduces law school exams and is not designed to cover the many strategies that could be employed to reach mastery. For a more nuanced consideration and deeper dive into exam strategies, there are a plethora of online courses and books on the topic. Do not wait until examination time to learn these new skills, however; otherwise there won't be enough time to use them effectively.

Student Story: Willingness to Change

Jeff was preparing for the bar exam when we bumped into each other in the hallway. He had just found out he earned one of the top grades in my Wills class, so I began asking him questions about his law school career—I always listen to high achievers to learn their strategies for success. He mentioned his main regret was his first semester of law school because that was the only time in his life when he earned low grades. When I asked him why he thought it had happened, he said, "Frankly, I approached law school half-assed, thinking it was going to be like college." Those first-semester grades motivated him to change his study habits and spend more time in the library, including weekends. At the end of our conversation, I asked Jeff if he would have worked harder during his first semester if he had read this book before law school. He said, "Probably not, because I had too much pride in my abilities." The moral to the story is to not be overly confident in your abilities and to be willing to make changes from day one.

ESSAY EXAMS

We apply law to facts. We don't apply feelings to facts.

SONIA SOTOMAYOR

The timed essay exam is the traditional and predominant assessment method used in legal education, and learning how to master this type of writing is the gateway to success. Several factors make law school essays different from high school and college essays: precision, application, inferences, balanced persuasion, organization, audience, and exam planning.

Precision is the competency requiring well-defined rules. This means staying close to the textbook or professor's formulation, recognizing variation creates the risk for error. **Application** requires using facts from the question by connecting them to the correct rules in a legally recognized manner—this one component is what separates the best answers from the others. **Inferences** are factual opinions or conclusions identified from the exam question, which are not explicitly mentioned in the question. **Balanced persuasion** presents the argument in a convincing manner yet also addresses significant problems with the argument. **Organization** is concerned with following a structure that makes sense to the legal reader. Understanding the skeptical reader is where the student appreciates the **audience**, which is a detached legal reader and not the professor. And finally there is **exam planning**, which involves strategies to use once the exam begins.

Precision

Legal terms are identified, defined, broken out into component parts (i.e., elements), and connected to any related laws. After grading thousands of law school essays, lack of precision is a significant reason students don't earn better grades. For many, failure to master this skill continues beyond the first year, resulting in some remaining stuck in the bottom half of the class. Also, when students fail to understand what is needed to improve, they often create a false narrative, with some telling me, "I guess I'm just a C+ student, but I will become a lawyer." Believing this lie makes self-improvement almost impossible.

The average student answer generally provides a basic rule statement that is accurate but not complete. For example, on a torts exam a student must state the rule "a battery is the intentional contact of another in a harmful or offensive manner." On a criminal law exam, "a burglary is the entering of a home of another at night." Average answers often use the IRAC formatting technique—discussed below—and adequate application. The root cause for their average performance is lack of precision—the essays fail to define all related and necessary legal terms. This doesn't mean defining obvious words like "is" or "the" but, instead, defining terms judges and lawyers are likely to consider important at trial. So why do many students struggle with precision? Because they never learned the law at a deep level, which requires a different way of studying. These students go into the exam believing they know the law, having put in many hours throughout the semester reading cases and legal supplements. As explained earlier, law school preparation is not about reading for long periods of time. It is about studying the right material the right way.

Let's examine more closely the battery example mentioned above. In addition to providing the correct rule for battery, an answer must also identify and define "intent, contact, and harmful or offensive" because these are the three essential elements in all tortious battery claims. There may be more elements depending on the exam question, but these three are always present. *Intent* is defined as someone who "desires or purposes to contact another, or someone who has knowledge to a substantial certainty that the contact will occur." *Contact* is then defined as "the physical touch of a human being to another person." And finally, *harmful or offensive* is defined to include "any contact that is deemed harmful or offensive by society." And going back to the burglary rule above, a good answer will define "entering," "home," and "nighttime"—the three elements for this crime.

By defining all elements, the student is more likely to address in their essay everything the professor is looking for on the exam. This isn't some odd academic exercise, but rather the same process lawyers use in preparing court documents or legal memorandum. In other words, a law school exam is helping students develop the real-world writing skills used by practicing attorneys. Imprecision isn't the only thing differentiating the average answer from the better answer, but it is almost always one of the more significant contributing factors.

Application

Application is the part of the exam in which the reasons—the rationale—for the essay's conclusion are discussed and analyzed. It is where the "why" question is addressed. This requires using relevant facts from the essay question and combining them with the relevant law, leading to a conclusion that makes logical sense. Imagine a legal argument that goes something like this: "He committed a battery because I say so." In a dictatorship this works, but anywhere else this form of argumentation is ridiculous. Yet this is exactly the form of argumentation some of the weakest students use—a conclusion but with no meaningful support.

The application section should be explicit, leaving nothing to the imagination. When a relevant fact does not appear in the student answer, then the fact, from the grader's perspective, does not exist. This is because the professor grades only what they see in the student answer, not what the student meant to but forgot to write. Prior to law school, many faculty would help students by filling missing gaps in an essay, deciphering what the student should have written in their answer. In law school and the practice of law, mind reading, divination, and reading of tea leaves are not valued skills.

Here is an example from defamation. Defamation occurs when the defendant makes a false and defamatory statement concerning the plaintiff to a third party. The rule statement includes five significant elements: defendant, plaintiff, communication to a third party, false statement, and defamatory statement. Each element is discussed in its own separate paragraph. When discussing the false statement element, the first sentence in the paragraph should state the issue: "The first element in defamation is determining whether Joe made a false statement when he claimed Bill murdered Brittney." The reader now knows exactly what is going to be discussed. The second sentence provides a definition for "false statement." In the third sentence the application begins. Here is a correct application sentence but one that can be improved: "Bill was in Mexico on the day Brittney was murdered, so it was impossible for Bill to have killed her." Think about this sentence for a moment. The facts are correct, but they don't EXPLICITLY tell the reader why or how they are false. The sentence expects the reader to IMPLICTLY follow the argument as to why Joe made a false statement. Now, let's add this next sentence to the application: "Bill was not anywhere near Britney on or at the time she was murdered, which means Joe's statement was false because one cannot be in two places at the same time." The final sentence, the conclusion, will read something like, "The first element to defamation is met."

Here is an example of a poor answer: "Joe made a false statement when he said Bill murdered Britney. Bill was in Mexico on the day Britney was murdered, so the first element of this tort is met." Notice the writer did not explain how the facts were connected to the falsity requirement. While the reader can infer there was a false statement, law school and bar exam essays require explicit statements rather than reliance on implicit understandings. In other words, explain everything to the reader and leave nothing to the reader's imagination. If it remains unwritten, then it also receives no credit on the exam.

Inferences

Inferences are part of the application section but warrant a separate discussion. An inference is a fact or proposition that is not provided in the essay question but is established by facts or propositions in the question using logical reasoning. In other words, an inference is an additional statement or legal conclusion placed into the essay and that reasonably follows from the facts provided in the question.

Imagine two people are behind closed doors in a room with no windows, when suddenly there is a loud noise from the room. A third person immediately rushes into the room and observes one person on the floor with a bleeding hole in his chest. The second person is holding a gun. Do you know whether the person holding the gun shot the other person? Well, the facts don't provide this detail. But we can logically infer, based on all the provided facts, the person holding the gun shot the other person. On a law school exam, this is exactly the kind of inference that should be made. However, be careful with speculation, which is the product of imagination and not logic. For example, suppose an answer to the above hypothetical states, "We don't know if he shot the person on the floor because there could have been an assassin in the ventilation system who shot him." Is it possible there was an assassin? Certainly. But based on the provided facts, there is no reason to believe the assassin narrative. Stating that the person holding the gun shot the person on the ground is a logical inference, while asserting there was an assassin is speculation. On an exam, students who make logical inferences generally do well, while those who speculate leave the professor baffled.

Balanced Persuasion / Counter Arguments

Great student essays use persuasion effectively, balancing their arguments with relevant and realistic counter arguments. In this context, persuasion means picking a side. This occurs naturally when the essay question states something like, "Discuss the causes of action Jana is likely to bring." Other exam questions may state, "Discuss all issues raised by the facts." In the latter type of question, it is important to pick a side and then attempt to persuade the exam grader. Writing a persuasive essay is important because this is what lawyers do. In litigation, lawyers represent the plaintiff or defendant. When preparing a policy statement for a government agency or non-profit, lawyers advocate for a particular position (e.g., why NASA should send more spaceships to Mars or why the Red Cross should purchase more emergency temporary habitats). Persuasion on a law school essay exam is preparing students for the practice of law.

Now that we have discussed why persuasion is important, let's address how to do it well. This new skill is a mystery to many law students, so they default to what I call ping-pong argumentation. Students use this ineffective approach either because they don't know the law well or they read somewhere that good law school essays include counter arguments. While the better essays do use counter arguments, they do so at the right places. The ping-pong format goes something like this:

On issue one the plaintiff will argue this, but then the defendant will argue that. Plaintiff wins issue one. For issue two, plaintiff will argue this, but defendant will then argue that. Plaintiff wins issue two. On issue three plaintiff will argue this, but defendant will argue that.

This type of answer usually continues for the entire essay, making the exam grader dizzy with the back and forth on every issue.

Let's work through a concrete example to see how ridiculous the ping-pong format is at times. Imagine this essay question:

Homeowner has a pet shark, which he keeps in a swimming pool in his backyard. Lucas was a guest at the home but got too close to the pool, not knowing there was a shark in the pool. He slipped on some water and fell into the pool, at which point his left hand was removed by the shark's teeth. Discuss all issues raised by these facts.

In this negligence fact pattern, the harm element must be addressed. Here is an example of a ping-pong answer:

The final element is harm. Harm occurs when the plaintiff suffers actual injury by the defendant. The plaintiff will argue he suffered harm when the defendant's pet shark bit his hand off. However, the defendant will argue there was no harm because he still has another hand. Plaintiff should prevail on the harm element.

The student stated the correct issue, rule, and excellent analysis for the plaintiff. But the counter argument is bizarre, including the conclusion the "plaintiff should prevail on the harm element." Really, "should prevail"? Any reasonable person would concede a hand removed by a shark qualifies as harm. So, why do some students write bizarre counter arguments? One, because they often don't know the law well enough to recognize good, bad, and ugly arguments, so instead they provide counter arguments for each element hoping something sticks. And two, they read somewhere that counter-arguments are necessary so they use them without any discrimination. Professors implicitly expect students to use discernment when writing an essay. Ping-pong arguments are ineffective and demonstrate to the professor the student's lack of understanding.

Counter arguments should be included at points in the essay where both plaintiff and defendant have reasonable arguments as to why they should prevail. In litigation, this is where the opposing sides will spend most of their time trying to persuade the jury as to why they have the stronger case. Ask yourself: Where are the two sides likely to clash at trial? Or, in a debate, where are the two people going to spend their allotted time? If the debate is on homelessness, the two sides are not going to debate whether homelessness exists—the debate will focus on a solution to the problem.

While it is possible there might be a good counter argument for each element, that isn't likely on an exam. It is more likely the facts in the essay question require only a counter argument for a few elements. In the pet shark hypothetical, both sides will clash around two issues: one, whether the guest should have gotten close to the pool; two, whether the home-owner should have warned the guest about the pet shark. If this hypothetical involved real litigation, the defendant would concede there was harm, he owned the pet shark, and he invited the guest to his home. Strange counter arguments hurt a case rather than help it. This requires a deep understanding of the underlying legal principles.

Organization: IRAC

Well-written essays are organized using a format that presents arguments in a logical and consistent manner. There are a myriad of formats, including BRAC, CREAC, IRAC, and IRAAC to name just a few of the dozens of available methods. The IRAC method is the oldest and most recommended method for law school essay exams, though one could follow any format recommended by the professor. The IRAC acronym stands for Issue, Rule, Application (or Analysis), and Conclusion. The use of an organizational system is not a magical talisman that automatically earns high grades, but not using IRAC or some other system will almost certainly result in lower grades. I have failed students who used IRAC but identified the wrong issues or used exceptionally weak arguments.

The IRAC method is a powerful tool because it forces a full exploration on every issue spotted by the student. But like any tool, it must be used correctly. This means using the nested-IRAC method, also called mini-IRACs. What follows next are some facts, which we will then use to nest a few IRACs together.

John owns several cows on a small farm. One day, one of the cows gets through a broken fence, which was damaged recently in a storm. The cow enters the land owned by Maria, eating many of her rare and expensive flowers. It is clear John acted reasonably in maintaining the fence.

This first paragraph is the topic paragraph, which explains to the reader what the essay is all about. Do not assume the reader knows the main issue or any of the facts; the essay must explain everything to the reader. The topic paragraph should include the two sides, the main issue, and the most important fact.

The issue is whether John is liable to Maria for strict liability when his cow ate her expensive flowers. Keepers of cattle are strictly liable when four elements are established: trespassing cattle, actual cause, proximate cause, and damages. Maria will prevail in her suit against John.

Notice how the paragraph above failed to provide any application of law to facts. This is intentional because the first paragraph is designed to introduce the reader to what follows. Think of it as a short summary, helping the reader by providing them with a roadmap to the essay.

Each paragraph that follows the topic paragraph should have at least four sentences: one for Issue, one or more for Rule, one or more for Application, and one for Conclusion. Use the paragraph structure to verify the answer is complete. When a paragraph has fewer than four sentences, something is missing.

The next section addresses the first element to this tort. As you read it, identify the IRAC structure, notice how it flows, and observe that nothing is left to the imagination.

The first element asks whether John's cow trespassed. Trespass occurs when someone's cow enters land belonging to another person. John's cow left John's farm, entered the land owned by Maria, and ate some expensive flowers. Even though John acted reasonably in maintaining his fence, this is irrelevant for strict liability torts. This element is met because John's cow entered Maria's land and ate her flowers.

The next section deals with actual cause, also called cause in fact. As you read it, ask yourself whether it makes sense, whether you have an idea of what this legal concept means, and whether relevant facts are used to reach a conclusion as to whether John is the actual cause of Maria's damages.

The second element deals with actual causation. A person is the actual cause of the plaintiff's injury when they are part of the causal link that resulted in the harm. Generally, the "but for" test is used in making this determination. Here, but for John's cow entering Maria's land, her flowers would not have been eaten by the cow. John is the actual cause of Maria's harm.

The final two elements are proximate cause and harm. Again, think about the format, identifying IRAC in each paragraph. Also, in the final paragraph, notice the overall conclusion to the tort for trespassing cattle—no need for a separate concluding paragraph.

The third element involves proximate cause. Proximate cause is present when the injury to the plaintiff is the foreseeable consequence of the defendant's action. It is foreseeable that a trespassing cow would eat vegetation, including Maria's flowers. The proximate cause element is met.

The final element is harm. Harm is measured by the damage done to the plaintiff's person or property. When John's cow ate the expensive flowers, Maria's property was destroyed. And the fact that the cow ate expensive flowers instead of inexpensive grass isn't relevant. Maria easily establishes the harm element. Because Maria can prove all four elements, she will prevail in a lawsuit against John.

Shortcut

Occasionally, there isn't enough time to write out the issue for each paragraph, especially when taking an issue spotter exam. In those situations, instead of an issue statement write out a word or two that describe what the paragraph is about. Use the word or phrase as a heading for the paragraph, using underline, bold, or quotation marks. For example, in the trespass paragraph, don't write, "The first element asks whether John's cow trespassed." Instead, write the heading Trespass. The issues in the next paragraphs can be reduced to Actual Cause, Proximate Cause, and Harm. The key is creating a plan for writing an essay at the beginning of the exam. But remain flexible. For instance, you might write the exam using this shortcut and, if time allows, go back and write out full sentences for each issue.

Audience

As with all communication it is important to understand the audience. A common mistake, though not an unreasonable one, is assuming the professor is the target audience. While it is true the professor grades the essays, thinking of the professor as the audience usually results in a lower grade. This occurs when students don't provide all the facts, details, law, or logical inferences, expecting the professor to fill the gaps in their essays. Before law school, one could earn top grades with these gaps because faculty filled them in. But in law school and in legal practice, failing to explain everything can result in lower grades or losing a case. To minimize this problem, it is best to write to a hypothetical reader.

The hypothetical reader has several characteristics. First, the reader is skeptical. They can be persuaded, which is accomplished by providing them with relevant facts connected to law. In other words, the hypothetical reader is persuaded by using IRAC. The essay should also have a logical flow, making it easier for the reader to accept the student's propositions. Third, do not try to figure out what conclusion the professor is looking for—that's almost always a fool's errand. Usually the professor does not have a "right" conclusion in mind. Instead, it is up to the student to pick one side or the other and then to argue for that side. What the professor is looking for are strong arguments, regardless of which side is selected by the student.

I recall a final exam where students could choose either the plaintiff or defendant, though the facts were stacked towards the plaintiff. All but one student chose the plaintiff. What I found interesting about the student who chose the defendant was that he fully supported his position, using facts to make his case. Although he made his job much more difficult by picking the harder side, he provided logical arguments for his position, which earned him an A. Again, it wasn't about the side he picked but how he crafted his arguments, using the right laws and relevant facts to reach a well-reasoned conclusion.

Finally, you could ask the professor what they are looking for on an exam. There are a multitude of possibilities, including in-depth analysis, ability to identify many issues, policy arguments, case names, and citations to statutes. The professor might not tell you, but then again, they might—"fortune favors the brave."

Exam Planning

When you are looking at an exam for the first time, it is important to create a strategy for tackling it before beginning to write.

Step 1: Determine how much time is allotted to answer each question. Usually, an exam will tell you how many points or how much time is available for each question. By way of example, suppose you have a three-hour exam. There are 30 multiple-choice questions, worth half of the total number of exam points, and three essay questions worth the remaining half. This means spending one and a half hours on each section, which works out to three minutes per multiple-choice question. For the essay component, this works out to 30 minutes for each essay.

Step 2: Keep time and stick to the plan, or risk running out of time. Many students don't have a plan and end up either not answering the last question or spending only a few minutes on it. When one section of the exam is completed faster than planned, the time can be banked for use elsewhere on the exam. But never borrow from an upcoming section of the exam to wrap up the current section—this will generally lead to not completing the final part of the exam. It is important to understand one does not have to earn a perfect score for each exam component to earn an "A" on the exam. So, instead of shooting for the moon, plan on providing solid "B" answers for each question. Generally, the student who does consistent "B" work for each question ends up getting a "A" on the exam. This is because the person who spent the greatest amount of time on one essay, earning a perfect score for that one essay, usually did sub-par work on the other questions. The key here is consistency: solid work for every part of the exam.

Step 3: Make a plan for each part of the exam. For a 30-minute essay question, spend the first six to eight minutes reading the question and then prewriting an answer. If a question has three parts to it, that means eight minutes total in prewriting—reading, organizing, and jotting down a few rules—and then about seven minutes for each issue on the exam. Studies indicate that students who do some prewriting outperform those who begin writing immediately after reading the question. The key is writing down a brief outline after reading the question and then following a plan.

Step 4: Never leave the exam room early—there are no prizes for leaving the exam early. If you get to the end of an exam with time to spare, then go back and review your answer. Make revisions to help the essay appear more professional.

Brain Dump

A common mistake on law school exams, which hearkens back to college exams, is to write down every rule statement one knows. In college, most professors rewarded student exam answers that provided lots of information. This is because college professors tested students primarily on knowledge retention. While law school essay exams do require knowledge of the law, this is the exam's foundation. Most points on a law school essay exam are allocated to applying the rules to the facts.

When professors see all these rules, called a "brain dump," we begin to wonder whether the student understands the issue or is simply throwing in everything they know because they are confused. For example, on a business associations exam the facts might state, "Matt is an employee." Some students then provide lengthy rule statements dealing with the level of control necessary to create vicarious liability. But that is unnecessary, as the facts provide Matt is an employee. By discussing control, the student has demonstrated they don't understand the issue. And when a professor is left wondering what the student knows, this generally means a lower grade. It is possible the student knew the rule, but because they discussed non-issues, employing the brain dump, they received a lower grade.

Another problem with brain dumps is the inclusion of rules that appear to conflict with each other. This often results in lower grades because the professor is confused as to what is and isn't known by the student. The solution is to place each rule into its own paragraph, with the format clarifying which rules apply to which facts.

A third problem occurs when the relevant rule is hidden among several superfluous rules, with the professor possibly missing the correct rule or not appreciating how the correct rule should be applied to the facts. Law school is primarily a professional school, which means preparation to become a lawyer rather than an academic.

When bringing a case before a judge, or discussing it with another lawyer, the judge or other lawyer wants to hear about the law relevant to the case—not everything you happen to know about the law. Judges, partners, AND professors are busy people, so provide only the rules needed to answer the question. Finally, since all exams have a time limit, precious time is wasted discussing rules that, at best, will be ignored or, at worst, will cost you points.

Student Story: English Major Problems

Lydia was an English major before coming to law school. After a lackluster performance on the final exam, she came by the office to get feedback. This happened early in my teaching career, so I made the mistake of saying her essay-writing skills were weak. She got defensive, explaining to me she was an English major and had written many essays in college. I no longer make this mistake but instead provide examples from the student's essay where they could have written a legally compelling argument. Lydia's problem going into the exam was not appreciating the difference between law school essays and the essay form she had used in the past. To use the familiar analogy, while apples and oranges are both fruit, they are different.

A few majors can hinder someone's law school journey. First, English majors, just like Lydia, can struggle. Second, journalism majors can struggle because they were taught to be as concise as possible. For them, I tell them to be *more* verbose—the opposite of how they were trained in college. Third, paralegals often struggle in law school, at least in the first semester. Their challenge is often pride, believing they have a huge advantage over everyone else because they worked at a law firm and took paralegal courses. Knowing about the practice of law is not the same as knowing how to practice law. Think of it as learning to swim in a kiddie pool and then being thrown into the middle of the Pacific ocean. My advice to paralegals is to second-guess themselves and pretend they don't know anything. In other words, take steps to avoid the illusion of knowledge. These are broad characterizations and many with these backgrounds are successful.

Brain Insight: Prewriting Predicts Better Outcomes

Many students believe they mustn't "waste" time organizing and doing some prewriting on a timed essay exam. So what they do is open the exam, read the question, and immediately begin writing. One study decided to measure whether prewriting was more effective than just starting to write, with researchers examining 890 timed essay exams.[10] Essays received one of the following three grades: distinction, pass, and needs work. In the distinction and pass categories, students who spent time prewriting outperformed those who did not; the needs work category did not show any difference. Note there were students who did well without prewriting. Interestingly, major revisions were correlated to lower scores. My recommendation is to prewrite, to not attempt major revisions, and to make revisions only if you decide you are done and are planning to leave the exam room early.

TYPES OF ESSAY EXAMS

It always seems impossible until it is done.

NELSON MANDELA

There are three major types of essay questions: issue spotter, analytical (bar exam), and policy. Depending on the question type, there are two fundamentally different approaches to writing an essay. The issue spotter question commonly requires very little application of facts to law, while the analytical style question requires a more thorough application section. Next, depending on the type of question, there are different essay-writing strategies. In an ideal world, the professor releases a few prior exams, which are reviewed early in the semester to get a sense of the professor's assessment methodology. Examples of all three types of final exam appear in Appendix 3.

The issue spotter exam, as the name implies, requires spotting many issues from a varied but loosely connected set of facts. This makes it challenging, usually impossible, to spot all the exam issues. The rationale for this type of exam is the careful listening required when interviewing a client, who may share a rambling story with lots of legal issues. Though all the issues are unlikely to be litigated, an attorney must spot them all and decide which issues should proceed in a lawsuit. One professor, who uses this approach, told me his best students spot only 75% of the issues. He also noted they don't all spot the same issues. It's impossible to spot every issue because of facts that give rise to theoretical issues rather than practical issues. Theoretical issues appear on law school exams and rarely get litigated in practice. Next, because of the many issues, it is impractical to provide a thorough application for each issue. Given the large number of issues, the best strategy is to spot as many issues as possible and provide some analysis. If there is time to provide a better application section on some of the more important issues, then do that. But rarely is there enough time to provide a high-level application section for each issue on an issue spotter exam.

When grading this type of exam, the professor uses a checklist, assigning a few points for each spotted issue—one point might be awarded for merely spotting the issue, two points for providing some analysis, and three points for exceptional analysis. Be mindful that professors are idiosyncratic, making it impossible to provide the grading methodology used by every faculty member.

An analytical (bar exam) style question generally requires spotting three to five issues, with the expectation of thoroughly analyzing each issue and sub-issue. The questions tend to be about one page long, with approximately thirty minutes to an hour per essay—the same as on most bar exams. The professor will generally expect definitions for legally relevant terms, often with each element getting its own paragraph using IRAC. When grading this type of exam, the professor has designed it to allow students to spot the main issues, with most points allocated to the application section.

One important variation on the bar exam-style question deals with the exam's length. The exam question might be several pages long, with the professor allowing three hours to answer the question. By question, I mean something broad, such as "please discuss all issues reasonably raised by these facts." The professor still expects the detailed analysis required for a bar exam-style question, but instead of three to five issues, the professor will have many more issues, requiring a thorough analysis.

The last type of essay question involves public policy, which can be embedded into one of the types of essay questions mentioned earlier or be written as a standalone question. Public policy questions are inherently subjective, where there is rarely a right or wrong answer. With this type of question, the professor is looking for a response that demonstrates an understanding of how the law might be applied, using societal, economic, or political considerations. In a Constitutional law exam, for example, the professor might expect a policy response to a question implicating an area with some level of ambiguity. Or a professor might prepare a standalone question, expecting students to demonstrate their creativity in providing an answer to an unexpected policy concern.

Student Story: Using the Professor's Words

Rebecca's classes were recorded, so she decided to use the recordings to help her improve her final exam performance. At times during the recording she noticed the professor repeated a rule or pointed out where in a case the rule was mentioned. During class she didn't have time to write down exactly what the professor said. So after class she went to the exact place where the professor had stated the rule and transcribed the professor's exact words into her study outline. This strategy allowed her to earn top grades.

One reason using the professor's own words improves exam performance is due to confirmation bias. When the professor sees his or her exact words, their mind is predisposed to think more favorably about that essay—an unconscious attraction by the professor to their own words. While this can result in a slightly higher grade, don't expect this approach to take an otherwise weak answer to the top. Think of this as a grade enhancer, which might move an exam from the tenth best to the sixth best.

Brain Insight: Practice in the Exam Room

When possible, study for an exam in the room where the exam is going to be administered. The two reasons are reduced anxiety and context-dependent memory. Many students struggle with anxiety, but it can get worse on exam day. This is due to several factors, including the high-stake nature of law school grades. But by studying in the exam room, you become familiar with the surroundings, training your mind to be comfortable in that room. The second reason takes advantage of the psychological effect of context-dependent memory, using location for encoding and retrieval. Most people have experienced this when they are in one room, walk to another room to get something, and then forget what they wanted in the second room. But when they go back to the first room, the location triggers what they wanted. "When events are represented in memory, contextual information is stored along with memory targets; the context can therefore cue memories containing that contextual information."[11] In effect, studying in the exam room can trigger legal principles learned in that room.

MULTIPLE-CHOICE QUESTIONS

I have not failed. I've just found 10,000 ways that won't work.

THOMAS EDISON

It is becoming more common for law professors to give bar exam-style multiple-choice questions on a final exam. These types of questions generally test higher-level thinking rather than knowledge. Do not expect questions like "battery includes which of the following elements," which measures only knowledge. A bar exam-style question is more challenging because there is often more than one correct answer, requiring the student to select the best option. And the best option might hinge on understanding one word at a deep level.

There are several reasons students don't perform well on multiple-choice questions, but the primary reason is students do not know the material as well as they think they do. Many students walk into an exam with a superficial understanding of the law, though they believe they have a strong command of the material—the same level of understanding that worked for them in the past. A student sees, for example, a question on a Torts exam and immediately recognizes the issue as "Negligence per se." This student does have a basic understanding of the concept: "a criminal statute or ordinance can be used to establish the standard of care." But the exam question requires a deeper look into the depths of Negligence per se, testing the student on whether the statute is applicable based on the nature of the plaintiff's injury. Because they never internalized the rule's intricacies, they aren't prepared to answer the question.

To do well on multiple-choice questions, one must practice. Unfortunately, most students don't practice in the most effective manner. What many do, including me when I was a student, is to read the multiple-choice question, read the four choices, reach a conclusion, and then look at the answer key. When the answer is correct, they move on to the next question without any additional thought on that question. And if it was wrong, they quickly read the provided explanation and think, "Ahh, that makes sense." This approach to practicing multiple-choice questions is marginally helpful, but there is a better way.

Significant improvement in understanding the law occurs by closely examining a multiple-choice question, dissecting each part. Let's use Appendix 6, Question 1 as an example. First, read the multiple-choice question without looking at the four answer choices and try to determine the legal issue based solely on the question. If using a book, place your hands over the four answer choices to avoid seeing them. Question 1 is relatively easy, and most law students spot battery. Second, go through the answer choices and find the right answer. Sure enough, battery is an option for Question 1. Often the correct answer presents itself because the student identified the legal issue before looking at the answer choices. The problem with looking at answer choices immediately after reading the question is you might start second-guessing yourself and head down the wrong path. Even if the correct answer is identified using these first two steps, the next step is essential for deep learning. Third, go through each of the answers and write down, in detail, why each of the wrong answers is wrong and why the right answer is correct. This includes not only stating the law but also the relevant facts in the question or answer choice. Also, capture your thought process as to why you think an answer choice is right or wrong. This final step is crucial because it's how you expose gaps in your knowledge and thought process. There are times when the right answer is selected through guessing or strong intuition, but that's not the same as understanding how the right answer was reached. By completing this final step, connections between different legal concepts are discovered and strengthened.

After completing these three steps, then, and only then, look at the answer key to see if your answer is correct. At first, even with one's best efforts, there will be several, if not many, wrong answers. Do not view incorrect answers as failure but instead as successes in identifying gaps in understanding. Also, slowly you will begin to discover the nuanced manner in which the questions are phrased, finding common patterns, which will help you identify those same patterns on future questions.

When beginning this work, focus on accuracy and not speed. This means using books, notes, and other resources. Once you start getting most of the answers correct, then move to completing them closed book. Keep in mind it might take you up to 30 minutes to complete one multiple-choice question with this method, but nothing valuable comes without time and effort. This method is designed to help you improve your multiple-choice competency and to learn the law at a deep level. And even if none of your professors give multiple-choice exams, this is still an excellent study method for learning the law.

Brain Insight: Testing Effect

It is well established that taking tests before a final exam improves performance on the final. One study delved deeper and examined three types of tests given before final exams: read only, multiple-choice question, and short answer.[12] Short-answer tests resulted in better outcomes on the final exam—not surprising because it avoids the issue of students guessing on multiple-choice questions. You can take advantage of the testing effect by completing the exercise mentioned above, forcing you to retrieve information from the brain and making a stronger neural connection to the law.

PRACTICE ESSAYS

Practice what you know, and it will help to make clear what now you do not know.

Rembrandt

Writing practice essays serves two purposes: one, as a means to master the law school essay format; two, as a way to learn the law at a deeper level by exposing gaps in one's knowledge. Some professors provide copies of their old exams, which provides insight into the type of exam they generally use. Unfortunately, a comprehensive final exam is not too useful at the beginning of the semester. Practicing essay writing skills should begin within two weeks of starting law school, starting with simple one-issue essays. These are also called short-answer questions and are found in several commercial study aids.

Because professors don't provide simple practice essays at the beginning of the semester, you will need a technique for creating practice essay questions. Learn to convert a multiple-choice question into an essay. Most multiple-choice questions test on only one issue, making them ideal sources for essay conversion. Also, there are multiple-choice questions that cover material already discussed in class. Each week find a new multiple-choice question and test your understanding of the prior week's material.

Now, let's see how this is done by converting Question 1 in Appendix 7 into a single-issue essay. After identifying the question and finding the right answer choice, what follows is a possible essay for Question 1:

The question is whether Peter has a battery action against Don after Peter's chair was pulled out from under him. A battery is the intentional contact of another in a harmful or offensive manner. Peter will prevail.

The first issue is whether Don had the intent to commit a battery. Intent is defined as the actor desiring the result or knowing to a substantial certainty the act will occur. Don walked over to Peter's chair, and as Peter was sitting down, he pulled it away. Don did this on his own volition, expecting Peter to fall down. Don's purposeful act establishes the intent element.

The second issue is whether there was contact. Contact is defined as occurring when the plaintiff is physically touched by some act committed by the defendant. When Don moved the chair, Peter fell on the floor, landing on his rear. Though Don did not directly touch Peter, indirect contact also qualifies. Here, Don knew the result of pulling the chair would be Peter falling down, which resulted in his rear making contact with the floor. This element is met.

The third issue is whether the contact was harmful or offensive. This is measured by what society deems as harmful and offensive. Peter was not harmed when he fell down, so that prong is not present. However, this element can still be met if the contact was offensive. Peter and Don were high school students, a time when seemingly harmless jokes might create great embarrassment. Not only did Peter fall down, but everyone in the class laughed for about a minute, creating great embarrassment. Though not stated in the facts, this type of event has led some to harm themselves because of the embarrassment. The offensive element is met. Because all the elements of battery are present, Peter will prevail on the battery claim.

Once a practice essay is complete, the remaining problem is getting meaningful feedback.

There are several ways of getting feedback from a practice essay. First, one could attempt to get feedback from the professor teaching the course. While this is possible, it is highly unlikely the professor will provide any feedback on an exam they did not write. Even getting feedback on an exam they did write is unusual. Professors generally don't get too involved in helping with exam writing skills because they are busy preparing for class and working on their scholarly agenda.

A second option is to contact an academic success professional (ASP), assuming the law school has someone assigned to this role. The challenge here is multifaceted. Generally, the ASP is highly qualified and motivated to help but is also overwhelmed with advising many students; the problem is law schools do not devote enough resources to fully staffing the ASP department. Because of the incredible workload, the ASP might not have much time to provide carefully tailored advice on a practice essay created by a student. Also, some ASPs are part time, maybe holding two roles at the law school.

A third possibility is to hire a private tutor. The main issue is cost, with the high hourly fees. This can be minimized by using law school tutors judiciously for developing study and exam writing skills, rather than as weekly accountability partners. Use a search engine to find a "law school tutor" and then examine their qualifications. Also, before committing to a tutor, find out what services they provide and how they provide them, and ask yourself whether they would be a good fit for you.

Fourth, find a "study buddy." This is probably one of the best ways for obtaining feedback, if a good feedback loop is established. First, find someone who is committed to essay writing improvement and is willing to commit time to this endeavor. Next, each study buddy will convert the same multiple-choice question into an essay. Then swap essays with the study buddy, with each person grading the other's essay. This entails printing it out, making notations on it, and explaining to the study buddy what they did right and wrong. Also, it is important to be brutally honest in the grading. You may be wondering, "Why not do this for my own practice essay?" Because, generally speaking, people are not good at critically evaluating their own work. This is why we need others to review and critique our work product. When you grade someone else's essay, you may spot a problem and then realize you made the same mistake. It's easier to be critical of someone else's work. Also, as you see the good and bad in the other person's essay, you begin developing stronger critical analytical skills, which you can then use when writing the next practice essay. This approach works only when both study buddies are fully committed to the approach.

Student Story: Top of the Class and Transfer

Charles entered law school with a desire to transfer to an elite law school after his first year. He knew this meant getting into the top of the class and working harder than he had in college. He had access to all my old exams, which he dutifully completed under timed conditions. After each practice test he came by my office, where we discussed the areas he found confusing. After several practice exams he understood Torts at a deep level, earning him an A in the class. Charles ended the year at the top of the class, and he successfully transferred to an elite law school.

A word of caution: Do not attend a law school unless you are willing to graduate from that school. Many first-year students attend their second choice law school with a plan to transfer up—few of them ever do. The problem is grades are outside your control. All you can control is yourself—not those around you, who are vying for the same top grades. You come to law school with certain knowledge, skills, and abilities. What you can do is improve, spending time on what matters to earn better grades. If you end up in the top 10% then consider transferring. Many who can transfer choose to not do so, unwilling to leave friends and opportunities, including moot court or law review.

Brain Insight: Use of Practice Questions

Researchers looked at law students at two law schools, comparing their study strategies with their law school grades.[13] The researchers created a checklist and asked students to answer yes or no to questions like "I read all assigned cases in the casebook," "I review my notes after class," and "I make my own outline using my notes, briefs, etc." They found better grades were positively correlated with "the ability to explain confusing concepts to classmates and using practice questions to study." They also found a negative correlation between good grades and "the inability to organize essay answers, difficulty writing rules on exams because of lack of practice, weak critical reading skills, and weak synthesis skills."[14]

MEMORIZATION

A photographic memory is of absolutely no use to you...without the ability to analyze that vast mass of facts between your ears.

PROFESSOR KINGSFIELD[15]

Law school requires learning voluminous amounts of knowledge, which invariable means memorizing rules. In property, by way of illustration, most students learn the Rule against Perpetuities: "No interest in land is good unless it must vest, if at all, not later than twenty-one years after some life in being at the creation of the interest." Now imagine needing to learn 20 to 40 pages of rules for each course. Memorization has a bad reputation because students generally use poor memorization techniques. The primary memorization technique used by most students involves reading the same material over and over again or writing down the legal rules on paper and then reading them multiple times. This approach worked for many before law school, when there was time to use less effective memorization tools. But now, there is too much information and not enough time. This requires using effective memorization techniques along with different learning methods.

Leitner Study Method (Flashcards)

The human brain has two primary memory storage depositories: working memory (i.e., short term memory) and long-term memory. Ideally, students need to move memories from working memory to long-term memory. Much of what is learned on one day is forgotten within 48 hours because memories are initially stored in working memory. Reinforcing new memories, by accessing them multiple times, helps move them from working memory to long-term memory. Because memories in the working memory disappear, when it is time to review course material from earlier in a course, the brain has to relearn it because most of the memories never migrated to long-term memory. Relearning is inefficient and a poor use of time.

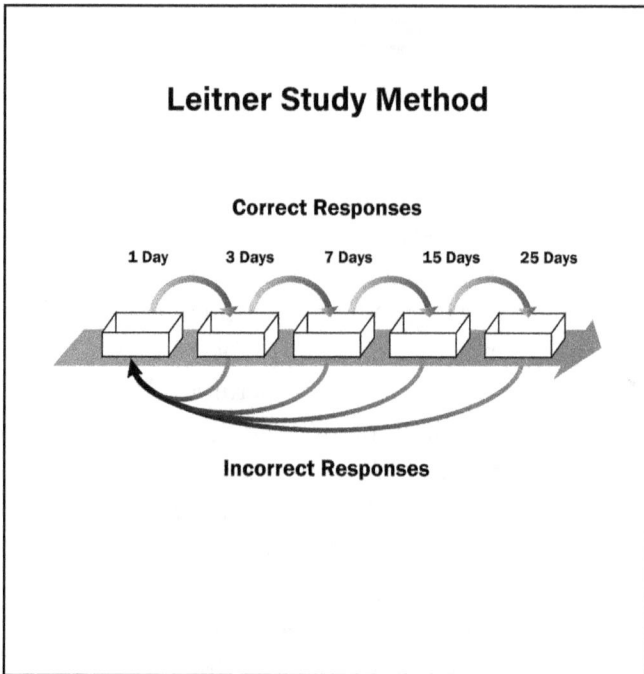

The Leitner study method is a way to use flashcards more efficiently. Most people learned to create one large stack of flashcards and then review every card in the stack at the same time—that's inefficient. The Leitner method involves first creating an initial set of flashcards, writing down rules or concepts on the front side of a note card and the definition on the back. For example, the front might say "Rule Against Perpetuities" and the back "no interest in land is good unless it must vest, if at all, not later than twenty-one years after some life in being at the creation of the interest." Keep creating flashcards throughout the semester. This method requires using at least five stacks, so have some way to store the stacks separately—boxes, plastic bags, or other containers. The first box is reviewed every day, the second box every three days, the third box every seven days, the fourth box every 15 days, and the fifth box every 25 days.

Every card begins in box one. Examine the card's front and then, without looking, state the rule that is on the back. If you have the first card memorized perfectly, then place it in the second box. If not, put the card down and place it back in the first box. Go through every card in the first box every day until it is empty. Every three days, work through the cards in the second box. The cards you have memorized perfectly go into the third box, but for cards you did not have memorized perfectly, they go back to the first box. Follow this process for the remaining three boxes, reviewing box three every seven days, box four every 15 days, and box five every 25 days. Reviewing boxes four and five is important in continuing to reinforce the memory, resulting in less memory loss. Incidentally, find a schedule that works for you. Maybe you need to review more often, so compress the schedule. You might also decide to add more boxes—there's nothing inherently special about five boxes.

When working through the flashcards, try to use as many of the five senses when learning. With flashcards, try writing them on paper or note cards, as this uses tactile learning. Typing is also tactile, but it often activates a different part of the brain and might be less useful. When possible, read them aloud. This uses the eyes and ears—two senses at once.

Finally, there are numerous flashcard apps you could consider. While this necessarily means not writing them out and thereby not using the touching sense, the app's convenience might be more useful. This way, when you have a few minutes of free time, pull out the app and work through a few flashcards—in law school, every minute counts.

Student Story: Exam Freeze

John was extremely anxious going into his closed-book final exams. After a poor final exam score, he came to talk to me. As we discussed his performance, John explained he was so anxious he froze several times during the exam, unable to remember anything from the course for minutes at a time. Memorizing a page of notes may have helped him unlock his memories during the exam.

Another possibility, at the start of a closed-book exam, is to engage in a quick brain dump before reading the questions. Brain dumping at this time will allow you to access any material stored in either short- or long-term memory, and it gets the action started to avoid anxiety or freezing once the "actual" exam begins (i.e., once you've read the question and have to answer it). This brain dump can later serve as your notes or outline when planning the actual answer. But if you use this approach, create only a high-level outline, capturing the big topics in the course.

REFLECTION

I thank God for my failures. Maybe not at the time but after some reflection. I never feel like a failure just because something I tried has failed.

DOLLY PARTON

Rather than simply moving on, the best students reflect on what they did right and wrong after receiving a grade. Unfortunately, most students accept the content paradigm versus the process paradigm. The content paradigm is the lie that someone isn't good in a particular area of law, with the student telling themselves, "I'm just not good at Contracts" or "I just didn't understand that professor." When someone accepts the lie, they essentially tell themselves that no matter what they do, they can't improve. On the other hand, the process paradigm recognizes weaknesses but works on developing the skills to become better—the journey of continuous improvement. The first type of student accepts their label, remaining a B or C student throughout law school; that's just who they think they are. The process-oriented student makes small, incremental changes, moving from C to C+ or from A- to A. The mistake is believing success isn't possible and continuing with ineffective study and exam strategies.

Reflection is essential for improvement, regardless of class rank. After a practice or graded exam, stop, reflect, and change so the next exam can be better. Identifying systemic writing problems should yield significant improvement on future exams, even in different courses with different professors. For example, a lower-than-expected grade may have little to do with the course content but instead with poor organization or failure to employ analytical reasoning.

From this point on I will refer to practice exams, but the process is the same for any graded essay. Step one is to complete a practice exam.

Second is to review, if available, the model answer or best student answer or to have a post-exam discussion with the professor or academic success professional. The third step, and the one usually ignored by students, is to spend time reflecting on what the essay did correctly and incorrectly. Reflection is a difficult analytical exercise that takes time to complete, but the more time invested yields a greater return on future assignments.

What follows are guided questions for a written self-reflection. Merely thinking about the answers to these questions rather than writing them down will not be too useful. For maximum effect, answer each of the first eight questions for each issue on the exam. For instance, suppose a practice exam involves Negligence, with one issue on the reasonably prudent person standard, a second on negligence per se, and a third on the eggshell plaintiff rule. With three issues, go through the eight questions for each issue, one set at a time.

Question 1. Write down each legal issue that should have been spotted.

Question 2. Compare the rules and definitions in your essay with the rules and definitions in the textbook. First, write out the rules from your essay, then write out the rules from the textbook (or model answer), and then explain either how your rule was perfect or how it could have been written differently. Also, if the rule from your essay wasn't perfect, write down the ways in which it wasn't perfect. Finally, write down whether you believe any differences were material deviations.

Question 3. Identify the facts from the question that your essay failed to mention but should have mentioned. Explain why they were not included in your essay.

Question 4. Identify facts you placed in your essay that were not adequately connected to the rule. Explain how they were not adequately connected and what you could have done differently to connect them.

Question 5. Identify inferences and conclusions that you did not provide in your essay and explain why they were not provided.

Question 6. How was your essay organized, and what improvements can you make?

Question 7. If you identified non-issues, discuss why you identified them and why they should not have been discussed.

Question 8. If you used unnecessary facts in the essay, discuss why they were not necessary and why you included them.

The next three questions deal with the entire essay and do not need to be answered for each issue. Answer these only once.

Question A. Discuss why missed issues were omitted.

Question B. Can grammar, spelling, or word choice be improved? Discuss and provide examples.

Question C. Was the exam completed within the required amount of time? If not, explain the reasons for not meeting the time expectation. Then provide a plan on what you will do differently on the next exam.

Generally, a detailed examination of these questions might take you an hour or more for each issue. But when you go through this reflection exercise, you will learn the law, exam writing, and the analytical skills needed for success at a deeper level. By way of analogy, imagine you purchase an exercise bike to strengthen your heart and a few other muscles in preparation for a very long bike ride you are scheduled to take in five months. Intellectually, you understand what you need to do to prepare. Every day you walk by the bike with that intellectual understanding, but you don't actually get on the bike. Finally, the day arrives for the long bike ride, and within a few miles you are exhausted, out of breath, and sore—you never make it to the finish line. Reflection is exercising the mental muscles needed to improve your law school performance.

The fourth and final step is to make changes. One excellent approach to reinforce self-reflection is to rewrite the essay under timed exam conditions. After rewriting the essay, go through the same three steps mentioned above. The goal behind this exercise is to train the mind to write differently. With the rewrite, the brain begins to develop better writing skills necessary for improvement. As noted at the beginning of this book: "Teach me, and I remember; involve me, and I learn." Reflection is about learning.

Student Story: From Failing to Top of the Class

Cole was a second-career law student who entered the law school's night program to improve his job opportunities. After flunking the midterm, he entered my office with a shocked and desperate look on his face. Cole was not someone who was used to failing and was willing to make whatever changes were necessary to succeed. Like many first-year students, Cole used the exam strategies that had worked well for him in the past. I provided him with the reflection questions mentioned above, which he answered in detail—several pages for each exam issue. This is exactly what Cole needed to help him understand law school exams, moving him from one of the worst midterm grades to one of the highest final exam grades.

Brain Insight: Retrieval Practice

"Retrieval practice (as occurs during testing) often produces greater learning and long-term retention than studying."[16] In the law school setting, many students will take one practice essay just before the final. Yet studies indicate multiple retrievals are better than one retrieval. Unfortunately, taking a practice exam without correct answers does little to nothing for students, which is why reflection is essential to help with learning.

STUDY SCHEDULE

Law is a jealous mistress and requires a long and constant
courtship. It is not to be won by trifling favors, but by lavish
homage.

JOSEPH STORY

It is essential to create a study schedule that works for you. It needs to be flexible but with a focus on what's important. In essence, a schedule is a self-accountability tool. Anyone who reads Benjamin Franklin's auto-biography realizes he didn't waste time. Franklin wrote, "Diligence is the mother of good luck." In other words, there is no such thing as good luck; rather, life's rewards go to those who remain conscientious rather than squandering their time. In Appendix 8 is a sample schedule to review while reading this section—notice the empty spaces, which provide free-dom in moving commitments when necessary.

A significant challenge in law school is the lack of time to complete everything to perfection. The saying "the best is the enemy of the good" means one must learn to create a good process because a perfect work product is often impossible given each day's competing demands. In law school and beyond, there will never be enough time—there is no perfect study outline, case brief, or Supreme Court brief. At the United States Office of the Solicitor General—where lawyers supervise the federal gov-ernment's litigation at the U.S. Supreme Court—there is a saying: "FIFI [file it and forget it]. When it comes time to turn in a project, lawyers often think 'if only I had a bit more time.'" Become comfortable with the good by creating processes that maximize the available time.

A good process is one that allocates time to what is most important. In law school, one of the most important goals is earning good grades, which is best accomplished by following the Master Study Cycle™. Spend time on these essential tasks: preparing for class, reviewing notes, drafting outlines, revising outlines, doing practice exams, creating final course outlines, and preparing for the final exam. These will never reach perfection because perfection in law school is an illusion.

First, place fixed commitments into the schedule. This includes classes, religious services, study group, commuting, and whatever else doesn't vary each week. Because they are fixed, there isn't a way to move them to some other time on the schedule.

Second, make sure the schedule is realistic. Some people create a schedule with every moment of the day mapped out. That works for some but not for most. The problem with a minute-by-minute, inflexible schedule is that most people become frustrated when something interrupts the schedule. There's nowhere to move the interrupted task, resulting in many completely abandoning scheduling. For example, suppose class is over at 2 pm with three hours before dinner. Someone might schedule Torts (2–3), Contracts (3–4), and Property (4–5). If scheduling every waking hour works for you, then great. If not, write Study Time (2–5). Next, create weekly and monthly goals. For weekly goals, consider something like "Exercise three hours," and for monthly goals, "Call Mom twice" (sorry, Mom, they should call you more often). This creates flexibility for the unexpected and results in your keeping commitments you've made to yourself.

Third, create a list of quick tasks you can complete during free time in the schedule. One possibility is to create three categories of quick tasks labeled A, B, and C. "A" priority tasks are extremely important, "B" priorities are moderately important, and "C" tasks are not too important. Imagine a one-hour break between two classes. After spending a few minutes reviewing notes after class, going to the bathroom, and grabbing a cup of coffee, you have 20 minutes of free time. There are no "A" tasks left, but you have a "B" task to check prices for a flight home for the holidays. In law school, every minute counts, and it is important to be as efficient as possible. Though if a classmate is talking to you, spend time with them too.

Third, create achievable goals. Don't write down things like getting the highest grade in Civil Procedure or getting the best grade on a test—these are outside your control and might lead to disappointment. Instead, goals should be process focused and might include joining a study group, completing four practice essays in Torts, talking to each professor about the exam in the first two weeks of the semester, spending an hour a week on self-care, or showing up to all classes five minutes early.

Fourth, write down the steps for each goal. These steps are placed into the schedule. Weekly goals might include 12 hours preparing for class, 10 hours reviewing notes, 2 hours preparing outlines, and 2 hours writing practice essays. Or, for the plan to meet with each professor, write down something like "go to Professor Johnson's office on September 3 at 1:30 pm during office hours."

Fifth, remain flexible. Rather than scheduling a specific time for each course, instead create a block of time called "class preparation" and then alternate from course to course. Generally, avoid spending more than one hour on a course—human brains need variety to maximize learning. During a two-hour study block, cover two or three courses with short breaks. In the upcoming chapter on Time Management is a detailed discussion on the Pomodoro Technique, a method that alternates between study and breaks; it is the method I used in writing this book.

Life's serendipity will interrupt the best schedule, which is why flexibility is essential. When the unexpected happens, shift what you were going to do to a different time. Don't get frustrated, but recognize that moving items on a schedule is normal. Some years ago I attended a Steven Covey time management workshop, and he said something profound: When you don't reschedule your time commitments, you are cheating yourself. This is because you had determined the task was important. If it's not important, then don't place it into the schedule.

Sixth, make time for yourself. Include breaks, exercise, cooking, laundry, entertainment, and talking to friends. The brain can't work at its optimal ability by studying for hours on end. Yes, you can force yourself to do that, but that doesn't mean you will actually learn much. Sitting at a desk reading without learning is merely the illusion of learning.

Seventh, once you create a plan and you've used it for a week, spend a few minutes at the end of the week reflecting on it. Ask what worked and what didn't work, and tweak it. This is your tool, so make sure it's working.

For many this is a completely new way of studying—it will feel uncomfortable. There will be a pull to go back to what worked in the past, which is natural. Think back to times when you had new experiences and what it took to get used to them. Maybe it was learning to ride a bike or water ski. Like those other experiences, this new study methodology can work, so give it time.

Let's move from the process of creating a schedule to the content—what you should be doing to prepare for class and exams. Many students never achieve their full potential because they aren't studying the right way. While grit, determination, and hard work are important for success, they are not the only factors necessary in law school. To help you understand, let's use the analogy of building a house.

Step 1: Foundation. This is the day before the first class of the week. First, read a hornbook, treatise, or study aid that explains the material that will be covered in class that week. Next, read the assigned cases. The reason for reading the study aid first is to provide context for understanding the cases. Be careful to not spend too much time on the cases, which takes away from the next few important steps. Third, brief the cases using the FIRAC case briefing method. And finally, take some notes on the reading as an active engagement strategy. Not laying a solid knowledge foundation is like a foolish person building a house on sand—the house collapses on exam day.

Step 2: Scaffolding. During class take notes on the law and any hints the professor provides about what might be on the exam. Do not prepare a verbatim transcript, as that is a waste of time. In a typical law school classroom, the professor is demonstrating how lawyers think through an issue, so taking notes at this point in the discussion is not useful. Instead, answer the professor's questions in your head. Don't write down everything the professor says, let alone student responses to the questions. If you leave class with more than one page of notes, you are probably taking too many notes. What the professor has done in class is create scaffolding to the foundation you laid on the day before class.

Step 3: Walls. Add the rules from the case briefs and class into the study outline. It is important to do this on the day of class because of the forgetting curve. The highest recall occurs just before and during class. But within 48 hours the vast majority of knowledge disappears from memory. Without reinforcing knowledge, it must be relearned before the exam. To retain the most essential parts of the classroom discussion, reinforce this material on the same day. This is why adding the rules to the study outline on this day is important. Also, don't correct the case briefs—that's a waste of time because case briefs are designed to help you prepare for class and nothing else. Now, repeat the steps under Step 1 for classes the next day. If there's time between classes, then work on the study outline then, or do some of tomorrow's class preparation during that time. What you are doing here is adding the walls to the foundation and scaffolding.

Step 4: Roof. This is the day after the last class of the week, which might be Friday or Saturday. First, review the study outlines on your own, making changes where needed. When they are perfect, then, and only then, compare your study outline to either a commercial outline or the outline of a student who aced the course in a prior year. But review only the rules that were covered in class, not material that hasn't been covered yet. And with this step, the house has a roof.

Step 5. Assessment. Now it's time to see how well the house was built. Without this step, there is no way of knowing whether the house is defective. Well, at least until the exam, which is too late. There are different ways to test one's understanding, but the two most common are multiple-choice questions and practice essays. This is, by far, one of the most important steps in the process and the reason many students don't improve. Many go into an exam believing they understand the material. Why? Because they have a superficial understanding of the material. The problem is they don't know what they don't know. The primary means of discovering hidden flaws in your home is to test it by throwing everything you've got at it. If it can weather multiple-choice questions and essay questions, it's a sturdy house ready to handle the storm.

Student Story: Success to Mediocrity

Zoe began law school by employing the study methods suggested in this book and earned high marks after her first semester. She came to see me after the second semester because she had experienced a precipitous drop in her grades. I asked what happened, and Zoe

explained she became complacent after the first semester, returning to her old study methods. She told me she believed her first-semester grades demonstrated her intelligence, allowing her to fall back on what had worked for her in college—it was easier and felt right to her. Beginning in her third semester of law school, Zoe went back to using the more effective methods, which helped her earn top grades during her first semester of law school.

Brain Insight: Schedules and Grades

Can scheduling result in better grades? Yes! Two University of Georgia researchers tracked college student grades over four years, taking into account their SAT scores. They found a positive correlation between grades and time management.[17] Their article noted the following:

> From our perspective the more interesting aspects of these results emerge through considering the factors as descriptions of behavior.... Subjects report feelings of being in charge of their own time. They are able to say "No" to people. They are able to stop unprofitable routines or activities.... [S]uch feelings of efficacy allow, and indeed support, more efficient cognitive processing, more positive effective responses, and more preserving behavior.

Follow the science and create weekly schedules.

PROFESSOR FEEDBACK

A professor can never better distinguish himself in his work than by encouraging a clever pupil, for the true discoveries are among them, as comets amongst the stars.

CARL LINNAEUS

Receiving individual feedback from your professor is important. Don't be afraid to ask for help with course content, study challenges, exam preparation, and exam grades. Professors typically post their office hours, so take them your questions or concerns. They want students to succeed but can get frustrated when a student hasn't done the preliminary work in preparing for the meeting or by asking simple questions readily found in the assigned material. For verbal learners, many professors do not understand that these students learn by repeating what has been said as a means of processing the information. They often misinterpret repetition as lack of preparation, so it is useful to explain why you repeat things. Now, let's discuss how to prepare for each type of meeting.

Course Content

Most legal concepts in a course are connected, so getting lost in one area will likely lead to broad confusion from that point forward. Some professors wait at the podium after class, which is a great time for students to get quick questions answered. But when you encounter problems between classes and have used the Dale Corson method mentioned earlier in "How to Study," then it's time to visit the professor. Try to eliminate any confusion before the meeting, maybe jotting down the exact questions you plan to ask.

Study Challenges

Most law school professors are not trained to answer academic success questions, but they often have useful advice. At a minimum, they should know who in the law school can help. At most law schools, study techniques and challenges are handled by an academic success professional.

Exam Preparation

Determining a professor's exam expectations is important. Professors generally provide some information concerning their exams, like the amount of time students have to complete it, what can and can't be brought into the exam room, and whether the exam is open or closed book. Some professors provide their old exams, which make great practice exams. If possible, take one of the professor's old exams and ask if they will review it with you. Many won't do that, but it can't hurt to ask. During a meeting ask the professor if they prefer policy discussions, citations to cases, citations to statutes, or citations to anything else covered during the course. The key is to gather as much intelligence as possible to help with your exam preparation.

Post-exam Feedback

There are many reasons to meet with the professor after an exam. First, professors do make technical mistakes, including making math errors on their score sheets, typing the incorrect grade into the system, or transposing exam numbers. I've made these mistakes, and other professors have too. The only reason these exam grades were corrected is students came to talk to me after the exam, and we discovered the error during the meeting. The worst mistake I ever made involved transposing two exam numbers. As discussed before, law professors receive exams with blind grading numbers rather than names. One semester I had two six-digit exam numbers that were very close to each other. Because they were similar, I posted the wrong grade into the system. When one of the students came for feedback, she told me the "C" in my class was the worst grade she had received. As I reviewed her exam, I found my mistake. She moved from a "C" to an "A." I then had to call the other student and tell him the bad news. So, when one course grade is an outlier, go talk to the professor in case there is a technical error.

The second reason to go see the professor is to get substantive feedback from the exam. After all, how can we learn from our mistakes if we don't know what we did wrong? Many students believe their grades are directly correlated with how well they knew the material—that is a fallacy for a significant number of students. After thousands of post-exam student meetings, the primary reason most didn't perform better is because they didn't know how to *write* a law school exam. I've even told students they would have earned an "A" if I had given oral exams, like they do in some parts of Eastern Europe.

When meeting with the professor, make it clear your objective is to learn from your mistakes and to receive feedback for improvement—this sets the right tone for the meeting. A common problem at post-exam meetings is student hostility, sometimes coupled with demands for changing grades. Resist getting defensive. Accept what the professor says at face value. Keep in mind most law schools have policies prohibiting professors from changing grades except for technical errors. There are times when professors review an exam with a student and realize they should have awarded additional points on some issue or were too generous on a different issue. But after exam grades are submitted to the administration, it is too late to make those changes, so understanding this reality will help the meeting go more smoothly. As you get feedback, take notes on what the professor says. If something the professor says doesn't make sense, ask for clarification. One good question to ask is "what could I have done differently to earn more points on this issue?" Some professors will provide examples, while others won't.

Most professors will not explain how they came up with the point values they assigned for a particular issue. Regardless, the points a professor assigns, at least implicitly, take into account the following four criteria: the rule's accuracy, analysis, organization, and writing conventions (e.g., grammar and spelling). When attempting to determine what happened on the exam, ask the professor questions to help you understand how they came up with a score for each issue. By way of illustration, suppose a professor explains you received 5 out of 10 points for the first issue—dig deeper. Follow up by asking what you could have done differently to get the 10 points. Listen carefully to the answer, as you may need to deconstruct the response to understand the exact nature of your deficiency. Was it a weak rule, poor analysis, or something else? If the professor says the rule statement was weak, probe a bit and figure out what a better rule statement looks like. Next, if the analysis was weak, ask what you might have done differently to earn the additional points. Throughout the conversation, listen for feedback that mentions weak organization, poor grammar, and spelling mistakes.

After grading thousands of essays, the vast majority of students follow the same pattern for every issue on the exam. For instance, when someone writes a weak rule statement on the first exam issue, they almost always write a weak rule statement for the second exam issue, the third, and so on. The purpose behind a post-exam debrief meeting is to get feedback, not to do a post-mortem on the exam. By understanding what you did well and poorly, then you can take steps to improve.

There are non-academic reasons for doing poorly on an exam: sickness, depression, anxiety, or interpersonal relationship difficulties. It is important to find help from the right person and to communicate significant issues with the law school. One student did poorly on one of my final exams because she took it when terribly sick. If she had spoken to the registrar, the exam could have been delayed by a few days. Then there are other problems, like running out of time on the exam. This is usually cured through taking more practice exams, though it might be related to anxiety, requiring help from a mental health provider.

If the primary exam problem is weak rule statements, there are several possibilities. One, you might not have known the law as well as you thought you did. The best solution is to complete the multiple-choice questions found in commercial study aids, following the process described earlier in the multiple-choice section. Over many years of teaching, I've noticed a strong correlation between students who do well on multiple-choice questions and those who have strong rule statements on their essays. This is because multiple-choice questions require a precise understanding of the law, which generally separates those who know the law from those who think they know the law.

A second reason involves inadequate rule statements. This is when students discuss only the basic rule, failing to mention necessary related sub-rules or to define legally relevant terms. This usually occurs because students expect professors to infer they know the rules they did not write in their essay.

Never assume the professor knows the law. In fact, only two assumptions can safely be made. First, the professor reads English, and second, the professor has a college education. One exercise that may help is to visualize the person who will read the essay. Pretend you are writing the exam for a favorite college teacher (i.e., someone who wasn't a lawyer). Imagine this favorite teacher waiting to read your essay as soon as it's complete. This teacher has neither seen the essay question nor knows the law. Whatever you want your teacher to know about the law or facts from the exam must be included in your essay—what's left unsaid is left ungraded.

Moving on to application, there are two reasons students don't do well. The first is that application builds on rule statements, so an essay with a weak rule statement will have less to build upon. For example, an essay may forget to define intent but otherwise defines the other elements to False Imprisonment. That missed element, or subpart, leads to a partially missing application section on the essay. The second reason is the essay does not explain the "why" behind an answer. As mentioned earlier, this is where the essay connects the law to the facts in the question. The best way to improve application is through completing practice exams. But it's not enough to do them. You also need feedback. This might come from best student answers, an academic success counselor, the professor, or a private law school tutor.

Meeting Process

Law professors are busy—preparing for class, researching, writing articles, and meeting their service requirements to the law school, university, and community. At many law schools, scholarship is the most important part of a professor's job, with the administration minimizing teaching competencies in favor of scholarship. With an understanding of faculty time constraints, let's discuss how to create a positive meeting experience.

First, be respectful. This should go without saying, but respect is a common courtesy shown to everyone from the janitor to the university president. Some students begin their interaction with a professor by making demands. Examples include "I must meet with you by the end of today" or "you must give me more points, so I don't lose my scholarship." The primary reason for meeting with a professor is to learn.

Second, meet with the professor during their posted office hours, or request a meeting outside of office hours, identifying the topic and amount of time you need—keep it to no more than 30 minutes. In the email subject line, write something like "Request for 30 minutes to discuss confusing topics." This is a reasonable request that is unlikely to be refused. If the professor counters with something shorter, then take it—a 15-minute meeting is better than no meeting.

Third, when meeting after the end of the semester, tell the professor you want a meeting to help improve your exam writing. Professors generally can't change grades, so don't alienate them by suggesting the purpose for a meeting is a grade reconsideration. Incidentally, while law schools normally have procedures to challenge grades, these appeals are almost always a waste of time. As one former colleague would tell his students who challenged him: "How long have you been grading law school exams, and what are your credentials for telling me my grading method is not fair?" That being said, if you can prove bias or arbitrary grading, then it is worth appealing. But with anonymous grading policies, even establishing bias doesn't prove the exam grading was biased.

Here is an example of the wrong kind of email to send: "Professor, I just got my grade back and I need to meet with you right away. Are you in your office, as there is no way I could have gotten this grade?" The right kind of email will read something like this: "Dear Professor, I just got my grade back from your Contracts class, and I am disappointed I did not do as well as I had hoped. I would like to schedule 30 minutes to meet with you so I can learn how to do better on future law school exams. I would appreciate some time as you teach other courses at the law school, and I want to make sure I don't make the same mistakes twice. Thank you for a great semester." There are some professors who won't meet with any students, so in those cases move on. Hopefully you will have least one professor who is willing to provide you feedback.

Student Story: Uncaring Professor

A few years ago I read the following comment on a website. It was disturbing then, just as it is now:

> As a 1L, I spent weeks trying to get a meeting or grading sheet to decipher the professor's markings on my first final of law school. I was especially disappointed, as this was my first opportunity for feedback on anything written in law school. The professor rudely informed me via e-mail that he did not need to explain his grading. I escalated the situation to one dean, and then another, and neither contacted the professor. Finally, I drafted a petition and got over 35 signatures from fellow 1Ls demanding some feedback, which did not have any impact either. I learned not to look back after taking a final.

Unfortunately, this story is common at some law schools. A former colleague, who visited for a year at a Top 50 law school, told me about a faculty member in the office next to his. This professor kept his door closed when he was in his office, and when students knocked on his door he ignored them. Another story comes from an elite law school, where the 1L faculty delegated post-exam meetings to one faculty member. After meeting with the delegated faculty member, a student at that law school emailed me. He was despondent and desperate after this professor looked at the exam and told him, "You're on the right track, just work harder." That was the only post-exam feedback he received, which was no feedback at all. Frankly, I'm not sure how students can learn without receiving some feedback on what they did wrong and how they can improve.

Brain Insight: Feedback and Academic Performance

It should come as no surprise that receiving written, specific, and detailed feedback is strongly correlated to academic improvement—exactly what is missing at many law schools. One study measured feedback by placing students into one of three groups: no feedback, computer-generated feedback, and detailed feedback written by the course professor. [18] "Descriptive feedback that conveys information on how one performs the task and details ways to overcome difficulties is far more effective than is evaluative feedback, which simply informs students about how well they did."[19]

STUDY GROUPS

Find a group of people who challenge and inspire you, spend a lot of time with them, and it will change your life.

AMY POEHLER

Study groups help with learning, and they provide community—remaining a loner in law school is not good for mental well-being. There is an ancient Japanese proverb that says, "None of us is as smart as all of us." Though study groups are generally useful, a poorly designed study group can lead to pooled ignorance. There are several advantages to study groups, including accountability. When each member has an assigned task, it is more likely to get done, as most people don't want to let the group down. Also, when discussing difficult concepts together, a member's explanation might make more sense than the way it was presented by the professor. Then there are times we say something in class that later seems stupid or embarrassing, and the study group provides emotional support.

Before creating or joining a study group, it is important to understand the dynamics that result in study group success or failure. First, limit the group to three or four people. Two people aren't enough to activate group synergies, and when there are more than four, some members don't participate fully. The members of the group should have similar goals, focus, and motivation. The primary focus is preparing for exams, not group therapy, where members complain about life's difficulties. Also, look for philosophical diversity in the group. If everyone is progressive or everyone is conservative, confirmation bias is likely to occur. Differences, discussed respectfully, challenge assumptions, leading to stronger intellectual understanding and better emotional intelligence.

Second, determine when and how often the group will meet. Meetings that last less than an hour will likely be too rushed, while those that meet much longer than an hour tend to lose focus. While some small groups meet every day after class, I think that's probably too often—one to three meetings a week are sufficient. As finals get closer, however, it makes sense to meet more often and for longer periods of time. A problem with not setting clear timeframes is meetings tend to lose their primary focus. That may work for some in the group, but others want to leave at the agreed-upon end time. If you feel guilty when leaving, say something like "it's our official end time, and I have something else on my schedule." By the way, if that "something else" on your schedule is studying contracts by yourself for an hour, that qualifies; items on your schedule are important, even if they involve only you.

Third, focus on discussing what is confusing, not necessarily recapping everything discussed in class. Without a clear mission, a study group can morph into a social group. While community is important, too much social interaction defeats the learning aspect that was the impetus behind creating the group. It's really not useful to start gossiping about other students and griping about professors.

Fourth, trade outlines. Before a meeting, decide which parts of the law each member is going to work on, and then at the meeting swap outlines. Everyone has to prepare their own outline, but by trading them one can expose gaps in understanding and discover errors they've made.

Fifth, decide as a group to work on the same practice exam, swap answers, and grade another member's essay using the format mentioned in the Practice Exam section. Discuss the practice exam after they have all been graded.

Sixth, eliminate distractions during the sessions. This means turning off phones or setting them to airplane mode. If someone has problems with this—some law students are addicted to technology—agree to place all the phones in the middle of the table to keep them from distracting the group.

Seventh, review the law by asking each other questions about the law. Consider making it a game, with two members on each side—competition could make it more fun. The study group might use flashcards, exposing knowledge gaps. The key is to focus on the rules of law likely to appear on the final exam.

And finally, divide the work evenly and in a way that each member knows exactly what they are responsible for.

Student Story: Quitting a Study Group

During law school orientation, Elena joined a study group. Elena met several times a week with her group, fully participating with the other members. She wasn't getting much out of the sessions but remained in the group because she believed it was essential to success. After first-semester grades were released, Elena was disappointed because she was at risk of academic dismissal. At this point she reevaluated everything she was doing, including her study group. She decided to leave the group, telling them the sessions were not helping her. The problem with this study group was it had become a support group, and the academic discussion was not helping. At the end of her second semester Elena earned higher grades and was not dismissed from law school.

Brain Insight: Groups and Grades

Researchers at the University of Washington were curious whether group participation improved individual grades. First, they created a test to measure individual performance. After placing students into small groups, they asked questions about their group experience. They found that two factors improved exam scores: comfort and equitable participation. When students felt comfortable in a group and the group was not dominated by one person, exam scores improved. If you find yourself in a group you don't like or where one person dominates, consider leaving and finding a new one. Or at least try to get the dominating personality to share the floor by creating rules on how long any one person may talk.

CRAMMING

*[It's] like cramming your way through school. You sometimes get
by, perhaps even get good grades, but if you don't pay the price day
in and day out, you'll never achieve true mastery of the subjects
you study or develop an educated mind.*

STEPHEN COVEY

Cramming is a study technique in which one attempts to place vast
amounts of knowledge into short-term memory a few days before an
exam. This method increases anxiety and stress, and, by this point in the
book, you know it is not recommended. But if you find yourself before an
exam not having implemented the Master Study Cycle™, then let's discuss
some cramming strategies to get you past the exam.

- Don't blame yourself for not being prepared. That's not going
  to help and will keep you from focusing on what's important,
  which is doing the best you can on the exam. Recognize that
  you're human and that this can happen to anyone. Write down
  a commitment to not let this happen again, and then start
  studying.
- Determine how much time you have before exam day and then
  schedule the remaining time. Include time for meals, study
  breaks, and sleep. Time is not on your side, so use the available
  time wisely.
- Examine the topics covered in the course and select the most
  important parts—those likely to appear on the test. You need
  to learn those portions well, so focus your time on those topics.
  It's too late to learn everything at this point, so the primary
  goal is doing the best that is possible.
- Use study aids. Find a commercial outline and review it
  carefully. While it's better to create your own outline, during

cramming mode this is one of the many compromises you must make. The reason a commercial outline is not as effective is because it doesn't allow you to work through the law on your own, as discussed earlier.

- The key to cramming is repetition. Keep reading and studying the topics you identified as important. And don't focus time and energy on trying to learn any one topic, unless you're convinced that it will appear on the exam. The goal now is "good enough."

- Use practice exams. If there is some time before the test, then take one of the professor's old practice exams. Don't go into the final exam without having some idea of what to expect. It's too late to take more than one or two, but it is important to have some familiarity with the type of exam you are about to take.

- Minimize distractions. Find someplace to study where you won't be disrupted. This could mean leaving the apartment and finding a quiet place to hole up. Some look for a coffee shop or library. What worked for me was the public library, since I could find a desk and not worry about friends coming around. Also, turn off your cell phone or, if necessary, leave it in your apartment. It's too easy to break from studying to surf the internet for a few minutes, which often turns into a few hours.

- Implement good time management skills. Consider using the Pomodoro technique, discussed in detail under the Time Management section of the book. In a nutshell, you alternate between 25-minute study sessions and 5-minute breaks. Repeat each cycle four times, then at the end of the fourth session take a 30-minute break.

- Take advantage of caffeine. Normally you should avoid taking stimulants to stay awake, but in cramming mode stimulants may be useful. This book cannot provide medical advice, so find something that works for you. This could mean drinking coffee, energy drinks, or sodas or nibbling on something to keep you from falling asleep. Think almonds, not candy bars.

- Study out of order. Most students review their notes in the order they appear. The brain doesn't work well this way, so start randomly, at different places, read for a bit, and then jump to another section.

- Study out loud. Talk, whisper, sing, yell, or read in a different accent. By vocalizing, you'll remember the material better as you use an additional sense: the eyes read, the mouth speaks, and the ears hear.
- Sleep. The body needs at least six hours of sleep before the exam. Studies demonstrate that people who don't get enough sleep do not perform at their optimal level.

Student Stories: Forgetting After an Exam

During the final exam period I saw Mark in the hallway. We engaged in some chitchat, which led to a legal discussion on a civil procedure topic—not a course I was teaching that semester. It was a rudimentary question, which he should have known, as he had taken his civil procedure final a few days earlier. After a few awkward seconds of silence, he told me, "Professor Baez, to be honest, that was three days ago—I've dumped everything from civil procedure and am preparing for my next final tomorrow." I appreciated Mark's candor, but it was disappointing to learn he had used the cramming method and forgotten a key civil procedure concept.

Brain Insight: Cramming, Grades, and Memory

Cramming is a technique that takes advantage of working memory, where knowledge is retained for a relatively short period of time. But as explained earlier in the discussion of the Forgetting Curve, this information deteriorates rapidly and is almost completely gone within 48 hours. In 2008 two researchers found an inverse relationship between cramming and learning—material crammed is not truly learned.[20] First, while in college you might never be tested again on the same material, law students must pass the bar exam before getting licensed. Second, given all the time spent learning the law, do you really want to forget most of it once the exam is over, or would you like to keep most of it for your future years in practice?

PREWRITE AN EXAM BEFORE SEEING IT

I do not know anyone who has got to the top without hard work. That is the recipe. It will not always get you to the top, but it should get you pretty near.

MARGARET THATCHER

An underutilized exam preparation strategy is prewriting the exam. Not the actual exam—you won't see that until exam day—but a close approximation will help expose gaps in your knowledge and may help you earn a higher grade. If it's an open-book exam, this approach can provide a significant advantage over those who don't use it.

There are a quantifiable number of topics that can appear on an exam—use this fact to your advantage. For each topic and sub-topic, create a model paragraph. In a property course, by way of example, adverse possession often appears on an exam. The elements to adverse possession are represented by the acronym CHOATE: Continuous, Hostile, Open, Actual, for the requisite period of Time, and Exclusive. With that, let's create a few model paragraphs, beginning with the opening paragraph for an adverse possession essay.

The issue is whether X can obtain title to Y's land through adverse possession. Adverse possession allows a person in possession of land to obtain valid title to the land when the possession is continuous, hostile, open, actual, exclusive, and meets the statute of limitations. X will / will not prevail.

Observe how this model answer uses X and Y, instead of actual names. On exam day, substitute the letters with the named parties in the exam question. Because this is the opening paragraph, the only parts of IRAC are Issue, Rule, and a quick Conclusion. Now, to the next paragraph.

The first issue is whether X's use was continuous. The adverse possessor must maintain continuous possession, though continuity remains between successive adverse possessors if they are in privity with each other. [APPLICATION SECTION]. X's use was / was not continuous.

Notice that this section includes a potential discussion on privity. If the exam doesn't implicate privity, then no need to discuss it in the application section. But imagine a question requiring a privity discussion. This is where to create an alternate path. Place a note explaining the normal path and the alternate path—an if/then comment. Path one is the regular and normal path, which in this example leads to hostile, but if privity appears then discuss that first. In other words, create a map. Organize the essay in advance. Here is one possibility.

[Privity alternative. Ignore and move to Hostile if privity absent.]

Though X's possession was not continuous, X can establish this element through privity. Privity is a relationship between two successive adverse possessors, established through inheritance, lease, or sale. When privity exists, the successor adverse possessor can tack his possession to the prior possessor's adverse possession. [APPLICATION SECTION]. X will [will not] be able to tack onto Z's adverse possession, thereby establishing [not establishing] continuous adverse possession.

As noted above, this section is required only when privity is at issue. Continue creating paragraphs and alternate paragraphs for every issue, using the rules from your study outline as a guide. By creating this document, you are preparing for the exam in a completely different way. This is more efficient than merely reading the study outline over and over again. In addition, rather than waiting for exam day to organize your thoughts, you are doing this in advance, when you are cool, calm, and collected— at least, more so than on exam day. Lastly, by engaging with your notes in this manner, you'll expose gaps in your knowledge—gaps you didn't know were there.

GRADES AND GRADING SYSTEMS

Work is that which you dislike doing but perform for the sake of external rewards. At school, this takes the form of grades. In society, it means money, status, privilege.

ABRAHAM MASLOW

Professors use different exam grading systems, and then they assign grades based on their law school's required grading curve. These two factors make earning top law school grades more challenging but not insurmountable. The key is focusing on what is within your control and ignoring the rest.

Understanding a professor's exam grading system provides an opportunity for exam preparation, at least when the system is provided to students. Unfortunately, there is no universal exam grading system. However, every grading system explicitly or implicitly recognizes four factors: rules, application, organization, and writing mechanics (i.e., spelling, grammar, and punctuation). Each professor weighs these factors differently, assigning points based on the professor's subjective belief on what is or is not important. One professor might ignore spelling errors, while another might assign 20% of the grade to spelling, at least implicitly. A former colleague began her career as a legal writing instructor, which explains why she assigned a lot of points to spelling on her exams. On my exams, over half of the points are assigned to application because this is the most important skill used by lawyers. When talking to a colleague, who gives issue spotter exams, I learned that most of his points are assigned to issue identification, with less than a third of the points going towards application. On one of his exams, he might have forty issues, with the best students spotting only thirty issues.

Few professors provide their grading criteria and score sheets, but it is possible to discern this information from old exams. Generally, issue spotter exams give more weight to spotting issues than to application. They almost have to because it is not possible to provide a well-reasoned answer to every issue under timed conditions. So when approaching this type of exam, spend more time at the beginning of the exam prewriting, jotting down each issue as you review the exam. Then, on the essay write down a short heading to identify the issue, the first sentence with the rule, and then a sentence or two in the application section, with a short conclusion. Repeat this for each issue on the exam. Breadth rather than depth is the approach. In contrast, a bar exam-style (i.e., analytical) exam is identifiable by each question having only a few issues. In this situation, the professor is looking for a thorough application section in which law and facts are discussed and appropriate inferences are made.

There are also external means for determining a professor's grading style. First, talk to some upper-level students who might have insight into how the professor grades. Second, whenever the professor mentions their grading philosophy in class, write it down. Third, approach the professor and discover what they are willing to share. Ask them whether their exams are full of issues, what their views on application are, and whether they prefer policy discussions.

After exams are graded, almost every law school requires professors to assign course grades based on the school's grading curve, which is generally published in the school's student manual. The Traditional Grading Curve forced most students into the center, where they received a "C." This system has generally disappeared in legal education.
Most law schools have moved to a Modified Grading Curve, where the median grade has moved from a "C" to something higher. The result is half the student body earning grades at the median or higher. This makes hiring a challenge for law firms as they can't easily compare grades across law schools. Schools with lower curves are then pressured by students to raise the median so they can compete for jobs.

The Elite Law School Curve, seen at top law schools, tends to be highly skewed towards the highest grades. In addition to having a high median, it is rare for students at these law schools to receive any low grades. But even here, there tends to be pressure from students to keep moving the median higher, all in the name of competition for jobs.

There are at least two reasons for mandatory curves. First, it forces

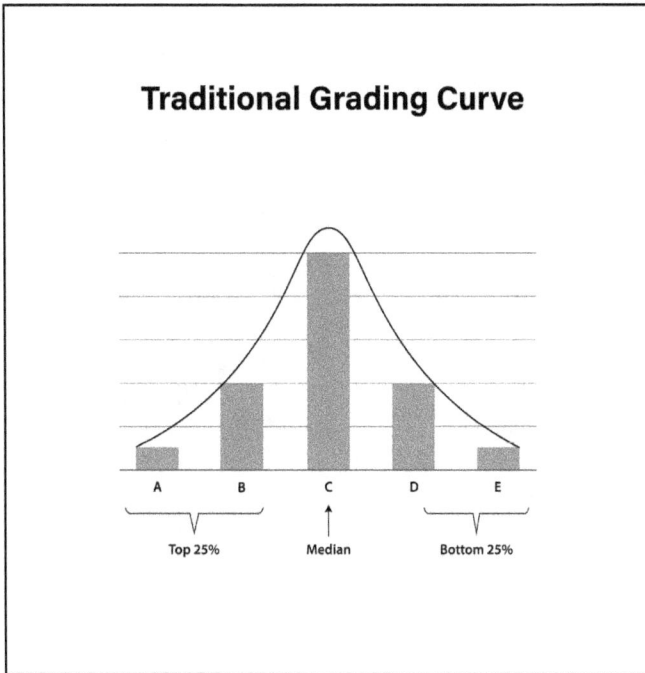

Traditional Grading Curve

tough graders to assign higher grades and easy graders to assign lower grades. At one law school, after grading the final exam and adding in other course assessments, I ranked students from highest to lowest. Based on past experience, I was inclined to award the lowest student a D- (almost a failing score). But after taking into account the law school's forced grading curve, everyone's grade was bumped up, and this student ended up with a C. The second reason for forced curves is equalization of grades between two sections of the same course taught by different professors. Depending on the law school, the policy might require an average course grade point average (GPA) or a forced distribution. With the average GPA, the grades must fall within a range agreed to by the faculty (e.g., between a 3.0 and 3.4 GPA). The forced distribution approach requires faculty to assign grades based on a grading schedule (e.g., 10% A to A-, 20% B+ to B-, etc.). What either approach demonstrates is the professor has no, or very little, flexibility in assigning grades—this is outside of your control.

Modified Grading Curve

A | A- | B+ | B | B- | C+ | C | C- | D+ and Lower

Top 25%   Median   Bottom 25%

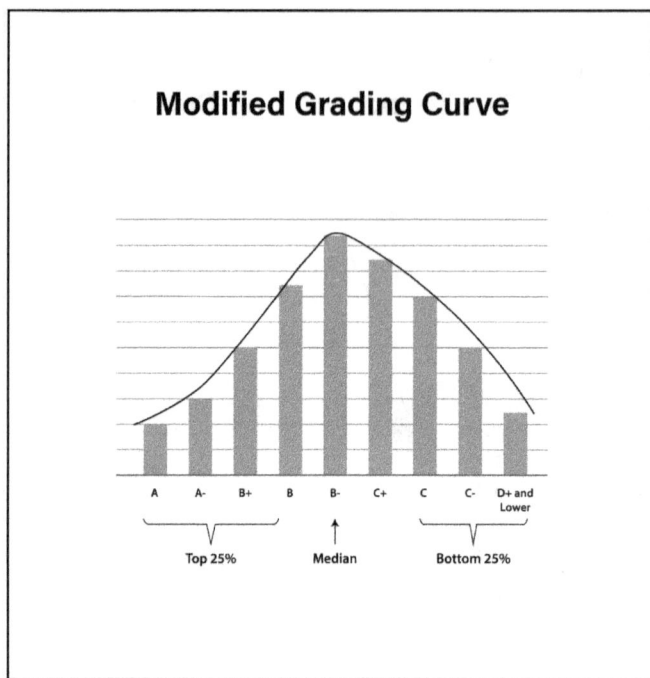

Student Story: Better Grades for Weaker Performance

One semester I taught all three sections of Torts—two day sections and one night section. I taught the courses identically, with the exact reading between sections and no significant differences in classroom discussion. The students received the same exam, which they took on the same day. After grading them, I noticed a difference in performance among the three sections. On average, one section scored highest, another a bit lower, and the third section significantly lower. My initial inclination was to rank the students from the three sections together, and then apply the law school's mandatory grade distribution policy. However, the administration opposed the idea, so I applied the mandatory grading system separately to each section. The effect of the law school's policy was to inflate the grades in the weaker section and lower the grades in the stronger section. From a student's perspective, the section they are placed into can make a difference in final course grade. Unfortunately, there isn't a way to find out if one section is, in fact, weaker than another. Also, students are

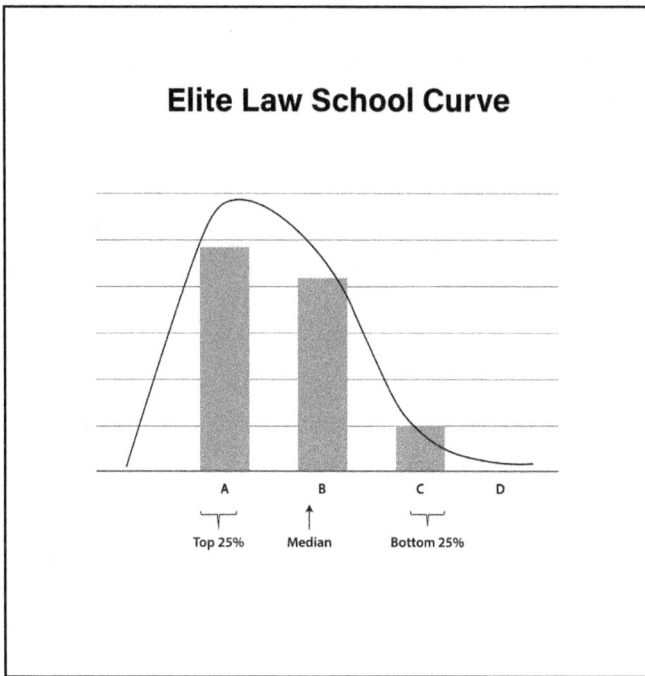

assigned to first-year sections, with almost no possibility of switching sections.

Brain Insight: Reliability of Essay Exams

In the early part of the twentieth century, Columbia Law School conducted an experiment to compare the reliability of law school essay exams ("old exams") with modern objective exams ("new exams").[21] This was a major endeavor by the law school faculty, which used more than a hundred "new exam" questions on their final exams along with "old exam" essay questions. They found the "new exams" to be more reliable than the essay exams, but more troubling was the correlation among professors grading the same students—not a weak correlation, but not strong either.

In plain English, this means student exam grades fluctuate more with essay questions than with "new exam" questions. By way of illustration, suppose Reginald was a first-year student who earned an A in Torts, a B in Contracts, a B in Property, and a C in Civil Procedure. There are a few possible explanations for Reginald's uneven performance. One, he knew Torts best and Civil Procedure least. Two, he was sick on the day he took the Civil Procedure exam. Or three, different professors don't write or grade exams the same way. Statistically speaking, the last option was the reason. They made this conclusion because the "new exam" questions were more reliable measurement tools than essay questions, which eliminated the possibility Reginald was sick or knew one topic better than the other. (This is a very simplistic discussion, so my apologies to those with a strong understanding in statistics.)

Practically, this equates to deviation in your law school grades. Even when you know all the course material well, due to idiosyncratic grading methods outside your control, you can't guarantee the same grade across all courses. Again, this doesn't mean law school essay exams are unreliable, just less reliable than more objective exams.

PART III: INWARD
JOURNEY

*There are three things extremely hard: steel, a diamond, and to
know oneself.*

Benjamin Franklin

Making changes to ourselves is difficult because it requires looking
inward and examining habits, trauma, hurts, compulsions, obses-
sions, or routines keeping us from becoming the best we can become. And
worse yet are the unconscious factors that constantly tug at us, keeping us
from our full potential. Inward struggles include addiction to drugs, alcohol, food, sex, pornography, work, or entertainment. Or our struggle
might manifest itself in codependency, procrastination, irrational fear,
panic attacks, unhealthy skepticism, inability to form deep relationships,
and a host of other issues. In one study of 12,000 lawyers, 20% had alcohol problems, 51% used sedatives, 47% smoked tobacco, 31% smoked
marijuana, 61% suffered from anxiety, 45% suffered from depression, and
11% reported suicidal thoughts at least once during their career.[22] The
more destructive habits can derail your chances of getting to the top of
the class or even graduating from law school.

    This book is not a self-help book, but does provide insight, techniques,
and resources to help you on your journey. The good news is the brain
can change, though it takes time and effort. The first and hardest step in
self-improvement is recognizing there is a problem, leaving denial behind.
Identifying your problems is not a sign of weakness but an act of courage.
And without this first step, growth and healing aren't possible.

    While it's true many law students and lawyers get by, or even succeed,
without ever addressing their internal struggles, they usually leave a path

of carnage in their wake. To illustrate, let's look at the life of Supreme Court Justice William O. Douglas (1898–1980). Though outwardly successful, he never managed to win his inward battle. He attended Columbia Law School, graduated second in his class, began his law school teaching career at Columbia, and then taught at Yale. Douglas left the academic life to chair the Securities and Exchange Commission and then made one final move to the Supreme Court of the United States at age 40. He was the longest-serving justice, authoring more opinions than any other justice. Yet his personal life was in shambles, with multiple romantic relationships, four marriages, and three divorces. One of his estranged children described him as "scary," and his second wife said he was "totally insecure." And concerning his Supreme Court opinions, they have been described as "drafts" rather than finished products. Imagine what Douglas could have accomplished if he had faced his inner self.

The American Bar Association's task force on lawyer well-being reported that legal professionals need balance in the following six dimensions[23]:

- **Intellectual:** Engaging in continuous learning and the pursuit of creative or intellectually challenging activities that foster ongoing development; monitoring cognitive wellness.
- **Emotional:** Recognizing the importance of emotions. Developing the ability to identify and manage our own emotions to support mental health, achieve goals, and inform decision making. Seeking help for mental health when needed.
- **Physical:** Striving for regular physical activity, proper diet and nutrition, sufficient sleep, and recovery; minimizing the use of addictive substances. Seeking help for physical health when needed.
- **Occupational:** Cultivating personal satisfaction, growth, and enrichment in work; financial stability.
- **Spiritual:** Developing a sense of meaningfulness and purpose in all aspects of life.
- **Social:** Developing a sense of connection, belonging, and a well-developed support network while also contributing to one's groups and communities.

Well-Being Balance

Intellectual Emotional Physical Occupational Spiritual Social

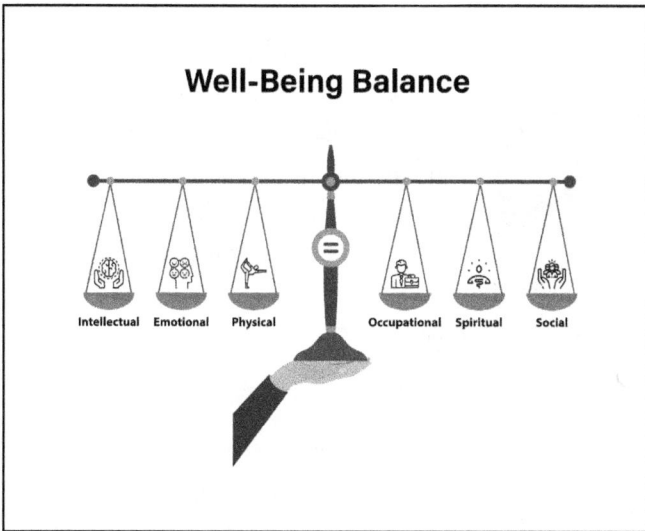

When one or more of these dimensions goes out of balance for any length of time—common in law school and the practice of law—then negative mental and physical issues can develop. I'm not talking about a few late-night study sessions, but rather regular and systematic neglect for months or even years. The answer to mental well-being lies not in finding time for each of these dimensions, but rather in making time for them—they are each essential.

Student Story: Abusive Marriage & Recovery

Lucy attended law school after leaving an abusive marriage. She understood recovery is a process of continuous improvement and not a quick fix—there is no one-week seminar to fix every problem. As part of her journey, she went to law school in a new and healthier relationship. She hired a life coach, who was helping Lucy develop stronger skills, like learning how to set healthy boundaries, be more assertive, and avoid procrastination. At the end of her first year of law school, Lucy ended up in the top quarter of the class.

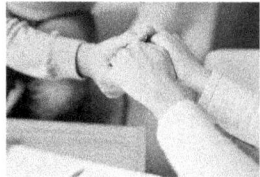

Brain Insight: Neuroplasticity

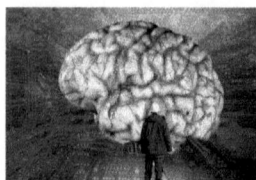

The human brain is plastic, meaning it can change and be molded after new experiences. For example, before attending law school, many are unable to appreciate legal reasoning. But after law school, the brain has changed the way it thinks to accommodate this new thinking pattern. Neurons in the brain are connected, generally following certain pathways. These pathways can be negative, as occurs with addictions—the person experiences something that triggers one neuron, and then additional neurons along the path lead to the behavior one is trying to avoid. But through new experiences, new pathways bypass old pathways. This doesn't mean the old pathway ceases to exist—they often remain there for life—but a new and better path is now possible.

CONCENTRATION

The lawyer is always in a hurry.

Plato

Concentration is all inside your head, and a number of factors threaten it. For example, you will often find your inner voice competing to take you elsewhere when you should be studying. Maybe it's thoughts about dinner, an evening out with friends, a trip you want to take to the Bahamas, your childhood pet, a relationship, and so on. Our inner voice cannot be stopped, and trying to repress it is psychologically dangerous. The problem is, when we hear the inner voice, it distracts us just long enough to get us to do something else, like go watch a video or spend time on social media. The solution is to recognize it, say something like "that's interesting," and then get back to your studies.

A second threat to concentration is sleep deprivation. Most experts recommend seven to eight hours of sleep a night, with studies showing a significant decrease in daytime concentration for those with poor sleep.[24] Additional factors that can negatively affect concentration are poor eating choices, lack of exercise, and use of certain legal and illegal drugs.

Pomodoro Technique

The Pomodoro technique is used to remain focused for long periods of time by using a timer to track study times and break times. It was created by Francesco Cirillo, an Italian college student who couldn't stay focused. He said the following:

> *Every day I went to school, attended classes, studied and went back home...feeling that I didn't really know what I'd been doing, that I'd been wasting my time.... It was clear to me that the high number of distractions and interruptions and the low level of*

concentration and motivation were at the root of the confusion I
was feeling. So I made a bet with myself, as helpful as it was
humiliating: Can you study—really study—for 10 minutes?[25]

Law students, lawyers, judges, and law professors struggle with staying focused, just like you might when your law professors assign more than a hundred pages of reading for the next day's classes. At first you might struggle with beginning the reading because it feels overwhelming. Once reading, you find yourself on autopilot, reading but not comprehending. The Pomodoro technique is a method that can help you stay on task.

Francesco was determined to learn to stay focused. He went home, sat down at the kitchen table, and grabbed a nearby timer, which happened to be in the shape of a tomato. (The Italian word for tomato is *pomodoro*.) He then forced himself to study in concentrated bursts, with small breaks between each study segment.

Here is his recommended approach.

- Decide which task you are going to work on.
- Set a timer for 25 minutes.
- Start the timer and continue working on the task for the set time.
- Stop when the timer goes off, place an X on a piece of paper, and take a five-minute break.
- After the break, go back to the second step and do another pomodoro. A pomodoro is each uninterrupted 25-minute session, so if something breaks the 25-minute session, you don't mark that down as a completed pomodoro—good intentions don't matter.
- Finally, when there are four X's on the piece of paper, take a longer, 30-minute break.

You might be wondering whether you need this technique if you already have the discipline to study for long periods of time. The answer is yes because it improves how much you can learn by reducing mental exhaustion. The brain needs breaks to process what it just read, so by taking short breaks more often rather than longer breaks every few hours, the

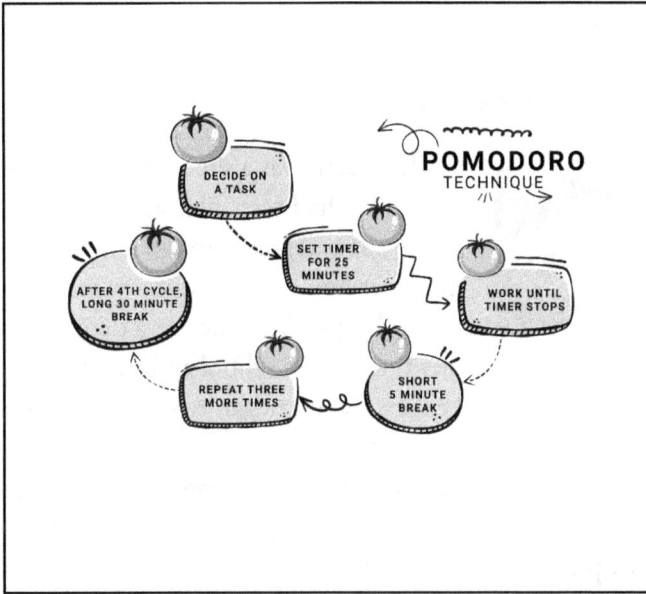

brain works more efficiently. You learn better and at a deeper level through this approach.

Francesco recommends using a manual kitchen timer, a piece of paper, and a pen or pencil. He believes picking up the timer and winding it by hand creates a psychological decision on your part to complete the task. From a behavioral perspective, you now associate setting the timer and working until the timer goes off, which strengthens your commitment to completing the task. The manual timer is what I prefer to use when in my home office.

There are also several paid or free apps you can download. The app I use at the university makes a ticking sound and also has a digital countdown or a rotating dial like a manual kitchen timer. Initially I thought the clicking sound would be distracting, but the sound helped me remain focused. The app also has a five-minute timer, which comes on automatically for break time.

As with any technique, it may or may not work for you. Some people love it, and others hate it. I recommend trying it for at least three weeks—don't give up right away. Most people notice a difference within a few days and mastery anywhere from one week to three weeks. If you own a kitchen timer, start with that, but if not, try a free time management app for a few days.

Student Story: Second Career

Elizabeth was a successful businesswoman in Australia, had teenagers at home, and was pursuing a law degree through a part-time program near her home. Like most law students, she was struggling with all the extra demands placed on her time by law school and the effort required to make sense of law school exams. As we began working together, one day she mentioned her struggles with remaining focused. I recommended the Pomodoro technique, and she immediately ordered a tomato kitchen timer. Over the next few years, during our tutoring sessions she would occasionally pull out the timer, reminding me she was still using this powerful method. The moral to this story is even successful people can develop new strategies to improve their performance.

Brain Insight: Effort-Recovery Model

Intuitively, we know breaks are important because we have a limited amount of energy, motivation, and concentration. But when should you take a break, how long should it be, how many should you take, and what should you do during a break? Under the effort-recovery model in understanding the role of breaks, our physical and psychological energy are seen as batteries that become depleted over time.[26] One study found that more short breaks helped workers recover faster than fewer short breaks.[27] This is exactly what the Pomodoro technique suggests—frequent short breaks.

But be careful what you do during your break. Many people are addicted to technology, so one temptation is to look at the smartphone during a break, maybe to catch up on social media. Don't do that. One study examined the question of whether using a smartphone during a break helps or hinders mental recovery. Interestingly, using a smartphone during a break hinders the restoration of full cognitive ability, thereby limiting the ability to study at the optimal level. This is because smartphone use is not actually a mental break, which means you are not "recharging" during the time you are using the smartphone.[28]

PROCRASTINATION & HABITS

You must always have faith in people. And, most importantly,
you must always have faith in yourself.

ELLE WOODS[29]

Procrastination is delaying or putting off something you know you need to do, instead doing something you know is not in your best interest. The ancient Greeks called it Akrasia, which can be translated as "self-indulgent." Common examples include endless hours on social media, binge-watching TV shows or movies, excessive workouts, and too much time spent socializing or sleeping. There are many reasons for procrastination, but often it's a conscious or subconscious avoidance technique.

Following are some ways you can avoid the problem of procrastination.

- Practice habit priming. This is when someone starts by completing the first step or two in a multistep process. For example, suppose someone wants to go on a long hike, which might feel overwhelming—the initial challenge is simply getting to the trail. To reduce the possibility of avoiding the hike, in the morning put on hiking clothes and shoes before going to school to study. By dressing for the hike, you have primed for the hike and are more likely to begin the task.
- Divide the project into smaller, manageable tasks instead of as a whole; otherwise, discouragement may set in. Ask yourself, "What are the first few steps I need to do to complete this activity?" For example, maybe you study best at the law school, but it's a Saturday morning and you would rather stay in bed. Literally, what are the first two steps to get to the law school? Step one is place your feet on the floor, step two is walk to the bathroom, step three is remove clothing before entering

shower, and so on. When you wake up, focus on getting your feet on the floor. Period. By breaking up the tasks this way you can ask yourself while lying in bed, "Can I get my feet out of bed and on the floor?" If you can't take the first step, read the section on Professional Counseling, as this might indicate a mental health issue like depression.

- Use the five-minute plan. When you realize you are avoiding a task, decide to work on it for just five minutes. When the five minutes are up, decide whether to do something else or keep going with what you are doing. Most people keep going.

- Create a deadline. Sometimes people procrastinate because they know they have lots of time before the task is due. For example, a final exam is coming up in sixty days, which means first creating an outline. Divide the outline into four parts and then create a deadline for part one in 14 days, part two in 28 days, part three in 42 days, and part four in 58 days.

- Make your plans public. While you might justify your lack of progress to yourself, you are less likely to lie to others. So if you have a significant other, give them your deadline. If you are posting on social media, publish the deadline online. Tell a friend at law school, who might become a study accountability partner. Creating accountability helps to keep you focused and working hard. I worked at one law school where the senior leadership team shared their goals during the weekly team meetings. No one wanted to fall behind, so we put the work into getting tasks done, even if it was the day before the meeting.

- Don't wait for perfection. In the words of Shakespeare, "Striving to better, oft we mar what's well." Many fail to get things done because they want perfection. But is perfection necessary? Probably not, so learn to live with good, and get it done.

- Just start working. For whatever reason, you may keep delaying the work. Decide you are going to start at a certain time and that you will work for a specific period of time. As you begin the task, you will get something done, versus just waiting for some magical sign.

- Go for a walk. It's possible the brain is exhausted and needs a mental break. A walk, some exercise, or even a movie may be what the brain needs to reset. The idea is to do something completely different from the task you are avoiding. This doesn't mean binge watching a show, but rather taking a short break to get you moving again.
- Stop worrying. Many people waste time worrying about a project, losing time they could have used working on the project.
- Think about why you procrastinate. Some are afraid of failure, so they delay starting or don't work hard. Have faith in yourself. Give it your all, so at the end of the day you know you at least tried. For others, there may be a fear of success. This is because truly successful people are rare in society, and many people find comfort in staying with the crowd. If what you are doing leads to success, you will figure out then how to handle it.

Student Story: Commuting Time

For a few years I commuted to the law school on public transportation. Several times I saw Amy, one of the law school's top students. The ride to the law school took 45 minutes, and I noticed Amy spent the entire time preparing for her classes. From the moment she sat down to the time she got off, Amy was reading her casebook. What I found interesting was her motivation and dedication, which I am convinced is how she ended up with excellent grades. Rather than using her commute as downtime to look at social media or listen to music, she was learning the law. Every minute counted for her.

Brain Insight: Habit Stacking

Habit stacking is a technique that leverages what you are already doing by adding something new to the routine. In the morning, for instance, you may have eight tasks you complete sequentially before leaving the house.

Suppose, after reading the advice in the Body section of this book, you want to add drinking 24 ounces (709 mL) of water each morning. Place this task at the end of your morning routine, which will make it easier to accomplish. Look for other habits in your day and then for opportunities to stack new tasks onto those routines.

WILLPOWER

*The most effective ... role of the will is not as a source of power ...
but as that function which ... can stimulate, regulate, and direct
all the other functions and forces of our being so that they may
lead us to our predetermined goal.*

ROBERTO ASSAGIOLI[30]

Lack of willpower is a problem for almost everyone. "If the will puts itself in direct opposition to the other psychological forces, such as the imagination, emotions, or drives, it will often be overpowered."[31] There are two common, opposing thoughts on the will. First, that it should be used to control our other functions, like when someone forces themselves to stop eating to lose weight or stop drinking to avoid getting drunk. Second, that one should ignore the will completely and just let the internal drives and desires have their way, as when someone exercises too much, takes drugs, or says yes to every sexual overture. The solution is to shape the will, developing skills to use it to manage our other functions.

Brain Science: Willpower Exercises

The following exercise for strengthening the will is recommended by Roberto Assagioli (photo on left), one of the pioneers in psychoanalysis, who studied with both Sigmund Freud and Carl Jung.

Understanding the Will [32]

Settle yourself into a comfortable position with your muscles relaxed.

A. Picture to yourself as vividly as possible the loss of opportunity, the damage, and the pain to yourself and others that has actually occurred, and that might again occur, as a result of the present lack of strength of your will. Examine these occasions, one by one, formulating them clearly, then make a list of them in writing. Allow the feelings these recollections and forecasts arouse to affect you intensely. Then let them evoke in you a strong urge to change this condition.

B. Picture to yourself as vividly as possible all the advantages that an effective will can bring to you; all the benefits, opportunities, and satisfactions that will come from it to yourself and others. Examine them carefully, one by one. Formulate them with clarity and write them down. Allow the feelings aroused by these anticipations to have full sway: the joy of the great possibilities that open up before you; the intense desire to realize them; the strong urge to begin at once.

C. Picture yourself vividly as being in possession of a strong will; see yourself walking with a firm and determined step, acting in every situation with decision, focused intention, and persistence; see yourself successfully resisting any attempt at intimidation and enticement; visualize yourself as you will be when you have attained inner and outer mastery.

After understanding more about the will, the next exercise is designed to provide you with more power over your will. Like the muscles in the body, the will can be strengthened through exercise.

Keep alive in yourself the faculty of making efforts by means of little useless exercises every day, that is to say, be systematically heroic every day in little unnecessary things; do something every other day, for the sole and simple reason that it is difficult and you would prefer not to do it, so that when the cruel hour of danger strikes, you will not be unnerved or unprepared. A self-discipline of this kind is similar to the insurance that one pays on one's house and on one's possessions. To pay the premium is not pleasant and possibly may never serve us, but should it happen that our house were burnt, the payment will save us from ruin. Similarly, the person who has accustomed himself steadily, day after day, to concentrating his attention, to will with energy, for instance, not to spend money on unnecessary things, will be well rewarded by his effort. When disasters occur, he will stand firm as a rock, even though faced on all sides by ruin, while his companions in distress will be swept aside as the chaff from the sieve.[33]

Before providing a few exercises, keep in mind that they, in and of themselves, are meaningless. They are designed to train the will. "The important thing is not the doing of this or that exercise, but the manner in which it is performed. It should be done willingly, with interest, with precision, with style."[34] Here are the exercises, though you could make up your own as well.

Each task or exercise has to be carried out for several days, usually a week, and then replaced by another in order to avoid monotony and the formation of a habit leading to automatic performance.

Resolution—Each day, for the next seven days, I will stand on a chair, here in my room, for ten consecutive minutes, and I will try to do so contentedly.

At the end of this ten-minute task, write down the sensations and the mental states you have experienced during that time. Do the same on each of the seven days.

Several other exercises of the same kind:

- Repeat quietly and aloud: "I will do this," keeping time with rhythmic movements of a stick or ruler for five minutes.
- Walk back and forth in a room, touching in turn, say, a clock on the mantelpiece and a particular pane of glass for five minutes.
- Listen to the ticking of a clock or watch, making some definite movements at every fifth tick.
- Get up and down from a chair 30 times.
- Replace in a box, very slowly and deliberately, one hundred matches or bits of paper. (This exercise is particularly adapted to combat impulsiveness.)
- Scatter 50 coins on the floor. Then quietly and slowly pick them up and place them in a pile. Do this once per day for several days, increasing the number of coins as you go.
- Take a book of at least 150 pages and turn the pages one by one quietly and slowly, making a pencil mark on each page as you go.

- Beginning with the number one, count out loud slowly and distinctly for 10 minutes.[35]

As mentioned earlier, create new exercises every week or two. Here is one I created a few days ago while traveling. At the airport I purchased gum before boarding my flight. As the plane was taxiing to the runway, I placed a piece of gum underneath my tongue, planning to chew it once the plane was off the ground. Due to weather issues, it was taking longer for the plane to take off. With the peppermint flavor in my mouth, I almost began to chew the gum. I stopped and decided to improve my willpower by counting slowly to one hundred. Even though the flavors from the gum were activating my taste buds, I ignored them and focused on counting. After reaching the goal I chewed the gum and appreciated the serendipitous willpower exercise.

MINDFULNESS

Who looks outside, dreams; who looks inside, awakes.

CARL JUNG

Mindfulness is living in the moment, not dwelling on the future or the past. Thinking about the future creates anxiety, while thinking about the past creates guilt. Also, mindfulness does not occur when we are on autopilot, which is when we are engaged in some task we've done thousands of times in the past, like taking a shower or driving to school, but not really being present in the activity.

Mindfulness is a type of meditation but not the kind involving mystics from India, emptying the mind, or sitting in the lotus position. Rather, it is a way of focusing on the now—the present moment—instead of all the thoughts constantly racing through the mind. First, let me tell you why it is important, and then let's practice with a short mindfulness exercise.

Our brains are full of neural connectors, which are firing at different times. Concentration is when we limit the firing of those neurons, focusing on one thought. Mindfulness helps us develop concentration skills, which we can use in the classroom, during studying, or on an exam.

Now let's try a mindfulness exercise. Assume a position that will be comfortable for three minutes. Next, set a timer for three minutes. During these three minutes you can close or not close your eyes—it's up to you. If you keep your eyes open, you don't want to pay attention to what you are watching—just keep your eyes looking at the same spot. While engaging in this technique you need an anchor—something to focus on. That anchor could be your breathing, your pulse, the wind, or some sound outside your home. When I did it earlier today, I closed my eyes while sitting on my office chair. The air conditioner was running, so I focused on that sound and made it my anchor.

As you focus on your anchor, your mind will begin to wander—this is natural. What you need to do when this happens is move your mind back to your anchor. You are practicing your concentration skills when you move your mind back, so don't get upset when your mind wanders—that helps improve your ability for compassion. From a scientific perspective, you are syncing your neurons to fire at the same time, thereby improving your concentration skills.

Student Story: Anxiety

Amber was a strong student but suffered from severe anxiety due to stress. During her final exams she would start to shut down because of panic attacks. Initially opposed to mindfulness techniques, she slowly began incorporating them into her routine. By her second year, Amber had fully embraced mindfulness, doing meditation exercises before her exams. This grounding technique significantly reduced her anxiety, allowing her to remain focused during her exams.

Brain Insight: Grounding Technique

Anxiousness is a common experience in law school, especially during an exam. This can be managed by finding a technique to bring yourself back to the present while you are sitting at a desk (though you can use this technique whenever you are anxious). This technique uses all the senses to reboot the brain, helping to create a sense of calm. Look at five different things intently for a few seconds. This could include a pen on the desk—examine its color, shape, size, and texture. Touch four things around you. This might mean rubbing your fingers on your shirt, feeling how soft it is, or maybe rubbing your toes on the inside of your shoes. Hear three sounds in the room. This could be the humming of air coming out of a vent, or someone walking down the hall. Smell two scents near you. This might mean lifting a wrist to your nose and smelling a slight bit of the soap you used that morning. And finally, taste what's inside the mouth. Maybe there is a slight taste of coffee. By this point you should be grounded in the present, helping to reduce anxiety. However, when in the throes of a severe anxiety attack, people often cannot sustain the mental focus to find, let alone focus on, five things they see or to name any traits about those things. They are too overwhelmed by the clutter of everything around them.

For an active and severe anxiety attack, simple, repetitive, and physical calming tasks might work better. Such simple activities may include turning over a clear bottle filled with glitter, tipping it back and forth, back and forth, in a rhythmic movement. Likewise, a snow globe or rain stick can also be helpful. Alternatively, an hourglass can be used, watching the sand sift back and forth, back and forth. By engaging in the physical repetitive movement of flipping an hourglass or glitter bottle, the body releases some tension, and one's breathing starts to match the cadence of the movement. Additional activities include tracing one's hand with the other hand's fingers or, if one likes, being a kid again and tracing the hand with a pencil on paper, matching one's breathing to the in and out of the fingers.

THE BODY

*Physical fitness is not only one of the most important keys to a
healthy body, it is the basis of dynamic and creative
intellectual activity.*

JOHN F. KENNEDY

Taking care of the body is a way to strengthen the brain's neural connectors, allowing for better learning and retaining information longer. Modern science is confirming what the ancients understood thousands of years ago: "In order for man to succeed in life, God provided him with two means, education and physical activity. Not separately, one for the soul and the other for the body, but for the two together. With these two means, man can attain perfection."[36]

Exercise has the primary effect of improving brain function and, secondarily, cardiovascular and muscle improvement.[37] In one long-running experiment at an Illinois high school, physical fitness was incorporated into the curriculum. The result was a 17% increase in reading and comprehension. At the same high school, students took an international math and science test, where the Asian countries typically outperform the rest of the world. The students at this American high school came in first for science and sixth for math in this worldwide competition. This and many other studies demonstrate a strong connection between physical fitness and academic achievement.

In additional to academic achievement, studies have found other beneficial results. People who exercise can lower depression, reduce violent tendencies, and help improve attention disorders. One inner city school that added a physical fitness component to their curriculum saw a significant decrease in fighting. These studies have been replicated at schools in good neighborhoods and disadvantaged neighborhoods. In other words, regardless of one's socio-economic condition or current class standing, one should see an improvement in their academic results by incorporating exercise into their routine. Personally, when I need to work through difficult legal material, I go hiking for a couple of hours.

To begin achieving some of these results, first get your heart rate up to 80–90% of its potential based on your age group. Second, exercise in the morning to obtain a positive effect on learning all day long. Third, for maximum effect, work on your most difficult material right after the workout. Fourth, try more complex exercises, as these provide even more benefits than simple ones, like running. Unfortunately, although ballroom dancing in the morning might be effective, it is unlikely you'll find a dance partner who wants to get up at 6 a.m. to do the salsa or tango— and the next-door neighbors would not be too happy either. You might, however, be able to attempt a more complex morning routine via online video workouts.

You may think there isn't enough time for exercise. But with a potential 20% increase in test scores, do you really not have the time to exercise? Begin exercising at a time that works for you. Early morning may not work, so maybe aim for afternoons or evenings. When I was in law school, the time that worked best for me was in the late afternoons right after class. Exercising every day may be too ambitious, so begin with two days a week. The first step is to start, and then add to the routine. Also, make sure to study your most challenging material right after the workout for maximum learning.

Another issue involves hydration. Most adults need to drink about 64 ounces (1,900 mL) a day for the brain to remain fully hydrated. When we get dehydrated, we become disoriented, as the brain is no longer operating at peak efficiency. In the morning, shortly after waking up, drink a large glass of water, as the brain loses around 20 ounces (600 mL) of liquid during the night due to sweat, breathing, and urination. One way of determining hydration levels is by looking at urine color—nearly clear is an indication of full hydration, with yellow indicating the need to drink water.

A significant struggle for law students is getting enough sleep. Seven to nine hours of uninterrupted sleep each night promotes healthy brain function. Some try to manage the increased workload through sleep deprivation, which works in the short run but not long term. There are only 24 hours in a day, which means one must learn to prioritize. Cutting back on sleep is not the solution, with one study indicating that sleep habits were significantly correlated to higher grades.[38]

Intermittent Fasting

People fast for various reasons. For some it's to lose weight, some to help with blood sugar, and for others to get closer to God. From an academic perspective fasting might help with mental clarity, allowing for greater focus, better classroom performance, more effective studying, and higher exam scores. Before attempting a fast, note this book was not written or reviewed by a medical professional. Every person is different, so before attempting a fast, seek advice from your physician.

A quick search on the Internet will reveal famous people who fast, including Twitter CEO Jack Dorsey, who eats only one meal a day. In the ancient world, Greek mathematician Pythagoras required his students to fast before coming to him because he thought they needed mental clarity to understand his complex ideas. Fasting has traditionally been associated with not eating and is defined in one dictionary as "abstinence from food, or a limiting of one's food." More recently, fasting has taken on a broader meaning to include abstinence from any number of things, including sex, drugs, alcohol, technology, or gaming. Fasting, in the traditional sense of abstaining from food, has been practiced for thousands of years and been incorporated into many religions. For example, Jesus, Mohammad, and Buddha all spoke to the power of fasting.

In layman's terms, here is the science behind fasting. The human body produces a chemical called dopamine. In the brain, dopamine is a neurotransmitter, which transfers information between nerve cells. Specifically, it is believed dopamine helps with motivational salience, moving us towards something desirable or away from something undesirable. For example, suppose you love chocolate. You see a box of chocolates in your home, and depending on your dopamine levels, you might not think much about it, or you might binge eat the entire box. The idea behind fasting is to reduce dopamine levels, allowing your brain to focus on something other than food or whatever you are fasting from. While this approach is recommended by some and is used therapeutically to help drug addicts, there are no studies confirming it works to improve mental clarity. What we have are many testimonials from those who claim they are more focused during a fast and from those who claim fasting has helped them to break bad habits. When I began intermittent fasting, I noticed increased mental focus.

There are different types of fasts, including intermittent, prolonged, water only, juice, or time restricted. The idea for getting mental clarity is to do something different from the typical modern diet of eating three meals a day and a few snacks between meals. An article in the New England Journal of Medicine states, "During periods of fasting, triglycerides are broken down to fatty acids and glycerol, which are used for energy. The liver converts fatty acids to ketone bodies, which provide a major source of energy for many tissues, especially the brain during fasting." In other words, the body shifts energy from digesting food to helping the brain.

I decided to try an intermittent fast, where I ate only once a day. I had dinner on the first evening and did not eat again for 24 hours. During the first 12 hours after eating, my body was burning energy from what I had eaten, but after that it began to burn fat. I was surprised by a few things. First, I wasn't hungry during breakfast and lunch time, only getting a bit hungry right before dinner. In the afternoon I normally get tired, but not on this day—I was alert and more focused all day long. I went to the gym and exercised for an hour and was surprised I was able to complete my three-mile walk in record time, shaving ten seconds off each mile. That evening I broke the fast with a cup of coffee, which tasted better than usual. I continued the fast the next day, again had more energy, and was more focused at work. On the third day I broke the fast by eating lunch— 17 hours after my last meal. Almost immediately I felt sluggish, and my mind was not as clear as it had been earlier in the day. I also had a strong desire to go home and take a short nap. I continued this intermittent fast for two weeks, only breaking it for a couple of social events. On the days I kept my fast, I continued to have more focus and mental clarity. One unexpected benefit was the loss of 10 pounds (4.5 kg). During this time, I did not change my caloric intake or exercise routine, yet my body lost weight. The science indicates this is because my body was able to burn stored fat more efficiently.

Student Story: From Binge Eating to Better Grades

Zach struggled with mental and physical challenges during his first two years of law school—he never felt like he belonged. At the beginning of his third year he had an epiphany, realizing he needed to make changes. After deep reflection he decided to see a nutritionist and join a twelve-step program. He overcame his binge-eating problem and became more outgoing. He then saw a massive improvement in his grades.

DISABILITY ACCOMMODATIONS

I can't change the direction of the wind, but I can adjust my sails
to always reach my destination.

JIMMY DEAN

Disability accommodations are designed to help create a level playing field for those with physical, mental, or cognitive disabilities. Without a reasonable accommodation, a law student might fail or receive lower grades. Thankfully, accommodating student disabilities is more common today than it was in the recent past. What follows are some general principles and approaches to disabilities; specific advice is impractical because each law school has more or fewer resources to accommodate a particular disability. Also, two law schools might address the same disability with two radically different accommodations. By way of illustration, one law school I taught at had handicap access buttons only for a few restrooms and classrooms in the building, while another had them only for the restrooms.

Keep in mind that getting a proper diagnosis for a learning disability can be costly and time consuming. For example, before receiving an ADHD or ADD diagnosis, a student must go through many different tests spanning a month or two. Then the professional has to create a comprehensive report, which takes time, and only then is the report provided to the school's disability office. The cost, which can reach into the thousands of dollars, is often paid out of a student's own pocket. Because of the amount of time involved, a student should start the diagnosis process long before a semester has begun or else risk going a whole semester unaccommodated, which can result in failing law school.

Let's discuss why someone might request an accommodation. Before law school, many with disabilities succeeded without an accommodation. But law school is different. Before law school, someone might have succeeded by spending more time than their classmates preparing for class. The game is different now. A typical law student spends 40 to 60 hours a week on their studies, which means coping strategies that worked in the past may not work during law school. Also, because first-year grades are very important, taking a wait-and-see approach might result in lower first-year grades. This might keep someone out of law review or moot court and could limit future employment opportunities. It is imperative to proactively request an accommodation from the start.

Depending on the disability, law schools have different possible accommodations. Keep in mind the law school decides, after reviewing an accommodation application, what they will and won't provide. When a student with a disability is investigating potential law schools, disability accommodations should be part of their selection strategy, as some law schools are more accommodating than others. In addition, a law student with a disability may choose to take a reduced course load as a form of "self-accommodation." With this in mind, a law student may choose to attend a school that has a part-time program so they aren't locked into a full-time schedule.

One common accommodation for some disabilities is more time on an exam. Imagine a student with severe arthritis, whose fingers cramp after writing too long. The law school might grant this student extra time to complete an exam. Or maybe someone has a cognitive disorder, where they read more slowly than most. If extra time is awarded, it works like this: on a three-hour exam, the law school might provide a student with time and a half for all exams. So instead of getting three hours to complete the exam, they get four and a half hours. In another scenario, instead of extra exam time, the law school might determine a student needs a "stop the clock" break. During a timed exam the proctor stops the clock periodically and allows the student to leave the room for a break, restarting the clock when the student returns.

Some students need to take an exam by themselves, to avoid sight or sound distractions related to their disability. The administration might use a spare office in the law school building for the exam, or a university office somewhere on campus that handles all accommodations.

For students who can't write quickly or can't follow the classroom conversation quickly enough, the law school might provide audiobooks or paid notetakers. The notetaker could be someone else taking the course, a law student not taking the course, or a student from another discipline. One student who received this accommodation told me the paid notetakers often did not provide useful notes. One semester I was told there was a paid notetaker in my class, so I volunteered to provide my notes to the student. I suspect many law professors might not share their class notes, but it can't hurt to ask. Instead of a paid notetaker, a student might receive permission to record the class. Most law professors ban class recordings for fear students won't discuss topics freely. To address this concern, a law school might require a student to destroy the recording within some period of time after the class is over.

Some professors ban all technology from their classrooms, including laptops. But depending on the disability, an accommodated student might receive permission to use a laptop for notetaking. One result, however, is the accommodated student will not keep their accommodation confidential as they might be the only one in the class allowed to use a laptop. To address this privacy concern, a few law schools now prohibit professors from banning laptops during class.

Accommodation requests are denied when they are not reasonable or create an undue administrative or financial burden on the law school. And whether an accommodation is considered reasonable is entirely up to the law school. One law school applicant's accommodation request was denied when she requested a latex-free environment, even though she could have died from the slightest exposure. Specifically, this student needed the law school to verify latex had not been used in the classroom for 48 hours before each class session. The problem is latex is ubiquitous, used in everyday products like erasers and balloons. There really wasn't a realistic means for the law school to grant this request as there was no way to verify other students would not bring latex into the classroom.

Law schools have processes for granting accommodations, which result in delays before an accommodation is approved, modified, or denied. Then there is the need for evidence from a qualified professional, with the law school usually wanting a recent diagnosis—generally not more than three years old. The challenges are in understanding what documentation the law school needs, getting it to them, getting them to understand the type of accommodation needed, and then waiting for an answer. There might be some back and forth, which is why you should try to start the process before law school begins. Also, the law school may have a short window each semester during which it accepts accommodation applications. If you miss the deadline, then you might have to wait another semester.

Students with physical disabilities generally find it easier than those with mental disabilities to get an accommodation. This is because physical disabilities are often easier to prove. Mental disabilities and cognitive impairments are where law schools struggle in providing appropriate accommodations. For example, some law students with severe anxiety seek an accommodation from being called on in class, even though this is standard practice at almost every law school. These requests are routinely denied because being called in class is part of the education. Some students might have a letter from a qualified medical professional requesting double time on exams, but the law school grants them only time and a half or instead grants them a "stop the clock" break. Unfortunately, the legal profession, by and large, is skeptical of mental disabilities. In law school, this manifests itself in a concern that students might fake a mental disability, get an accommodation, and receive an unfair advantage on exams.

Student Story: Dyslexia

Kaylee needed help preparing for her law school exams, and she wanted me to write a model answer for an old final exam her professor had provided to the class. I explained to her this would not help her and that she would learn more by taking the practice exam by herself—we could then work together to review her essay. That's when she explained she had severe dyslexia, and any practice test she took would make her worse off as she remembered the wrong answer, having reinforced it in writing. For her condition, she needed to see the right answers first, memorize those answers, and then she would be able to recreate the correct answers on an exam. The key is to understand how you learn and that an approach recommended in this book might not work for you, especially if you have a learning disability.

Brain Insight: Higher or Lower Grades

One concern in granting an accommodation is whether it will provide a student with an unfair advantage. Before proceeding, let me be clear that my intent is not to perpetuate the stereotype that all accommodated students receive an unfair advantage. While a few accommodated students likely receive an unfair advantage, for the vast majority of accommodated students their accommodations level out the playing field, allowing them to succeed. Some still flunk out. The answer to this concern is not well researched, though a 2003 study compared SAT score with course grades for accommodated college students.[39] Specifically, the researcher looked at students with learning disabilities (LD) and Attention Deficit Disorder (ADD). The study found that accommodations for those with LD were not positively correlated with better grades but that there was a significant grade increase for those with ADD.

Given that no two people are exactly the same, especially with cognitive disorders, there will be some unfairness when accommodating students. One semester, a student told me about his disability and the accommodation the law school provided. He had a physical problem with his eyes, where floaters might randomly appear, making it hard to see. The law school's accommodation officer granted this student extra time on each exam, even though the problem did not present itself on every exam. Yet he always took the extra time. As mentioned earlier, in the vast majority of cases, accommodations level the playing field. Outliers who receive an unfair advantage are the exception, not the rule.

MENTAL HEALTH

*Lawyers better remember they are human beings, and a human
being who hasn't periods of doubts and distresses and
disappointments must be a cabbage, not a human being.*

FELIX FRANKFURTER

Many in the legal profession suffer from significant mental health problems, with many problems starting in law school. There are two aspects of mental health to consider. First and foremost, work on maintaining good mental health to minimize the risk of significant mental health problems. And second, if you see something wrong in your life, admit it so you can begin the journey to wellness.

Most people know, at least intuitively, what it takes to stay mentally healthy. This includes eating well, getting enough sleep, connecting with friends, exercising, avoiding the big three (tobacco, alcohol, and drugs), getting sunlight, managing stress, and doing things you enjoy. But law school can lead to isolation—moving to a new city with no friends, eating fast food, smoking to manage stress, skipping exercise, and sleeping fewer hours to keep up with the work. The answer is to find balance by making time for important mental health activities. If you have to, place them into your schedule and do them, just like you would a contracts reading assignment. If you normally go to the gym for two hours a day, consider one hour every other day. Or if you normally go to the movies once a week, consider one movie a month. Maybe you attended religious services before law school; if so, continue going. Find the right balance.

Some enter law school with mental health challenges or develop them during law school. Recognition is the first step to recovery, otherwise the problems get worse over time. After admitting there is a problem, the next step is getting help. Some law schools, especially those connected to universities, tend to have internal mental health counselors—this is a great starting point. Some students don't get help for fear they will be reported to the bar, which they believe may keep them from practicing law. While this may have been true in the past, today most state bars prefer lawyers dealing with their mental health issues instead of hiding them.

Group Therapy

There are more than 200 mutual aid groups that help people work through their issues, generally through the use of group therapy. The advantage to this type of therapy is it's generally welcoming, supportive, nonjudgmental, and free. The most well-known group is Alcoholics Anonymous (AA), which created the twelve-step approach to helping members fight alcohol addiction. Most other groups, though not connected to AA, follow some version of the twelve steps.[40] These groups are not comprised of professional counselors but of volunteers who are also working through their own recovery.

Meetings usually begin with a presentation on some aspect of recovery and then move to small groups where people can share struggles and victories. Many find freedom in meeting others with the same struggles, discovering they are not alone. Though anonymity and confidentiality are important in these programs, there are no legal requirements for participants to keep information confidential, as they are not licensed professionals. With this one caveat, group therapy is often a good first step towards wholeness.

While many twelve-step groups focus on only one substance or behavior, others are broader and welcome people with a broad range of challenges. Here are a few groups and their focus:

Alcoholics Anonymous: "An international fellowship of men and women who have had a drinking problem. It is nonprofessional, self-supporting, multiracial, apolitical, and available almost everywhere. There are no age or education requirements. Membership is open to anyone who wants to do something about his or her drinking problem."[41]

Celebrate Recovery: "A Christ-centered, 12-step recovery program for anyone struggling with hurt, pain or addiction of any kind."[42]

Co-Dependents Anonymous: "A program of recovery from codependence, where each of us may share our experience, strength, and hope in our efforts to find freedom where there has been bondage and peace where there has been turmoil in our relationships with others and ourselves."[43]

Food Addicts in Recovery Anonymous: "Is a fellowship of individuals who, through shared experience and mutual support, are recovering from the disease of food addiction."[44]

Gamblers Anonymous: "A fellowship of men and women who share their experience, strength and hope with each other that they may solve their common problem and help others to recover from a gambling problem."[45]

Sex Addicts Anonymous: "Our primary purpose is to stop our addictive sexual behavior and to help others recover from sexual addiction."[46]

Workaholics Anonymous: "A fellowship of individuals who share their experience, strength, and hope with each other that they may solve their common problems and help others to recover from workaholism."[47]

For a comprehensive list, visit Wikipedia's page on twelve-step programs: https://en.wikipedia.org/wiki/List_of_twelve-step_groups.

Professional Counseling

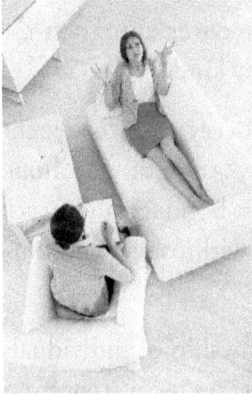

"Professional counseling is a professional relationship that empowers diverse individuals, families, and groups to accomplish mental health, wellness, education, and career goals."[48] Many have the false idea professional counseling is only for those with severe mental health issues. There are times when something just doesn't feel right, maybe a feeling of sadness, an addiction, procrastination, or anything else keeping you from reaching your full potential. Many law schools provide some free mental counseling support, either internally or externally. Sometimes we need someone to help us understand what is going on inside us, who can then help us get back on track. There is no shame in seeking help.

Student Story: Alcoholics Anonymous

After decades in low-paying jobs, Henry decided to attend college and then law school. Henry told me he grew up in a tough neighborhood in one of America's largest cities. It was the kind of neighborhood with many dysfunctional families, rampant alcohol abuse, and dead-end jobs. As a young man, Henry began to repeat the cycle through alcoholism and then a divorce after a few years of marriage. The divorce was a wakeup call for him, helping him understand he had a problem. Henry took that first brave step and went to his first Alcoholics Anonymous (AA) meeting. When he told me he was an alcoholic, I was initially surprised, until he added he hadn't touched alcohol in decades. During law school, Henry was actively engaged in learning, earned good grades, and had a solid plan for practicing law after graduation. He told me he was still involved in AA because he would always be in recovery, and he wanted to give back to the younger men in the program. That first step of going to an AA meeting changed Henry's life, allowing him to get out of the cycle that still has a hold on his ex-wife and the rest of his family.

Brain Insight: Mental Health and Grades

Mental health can affect grades and result in someone not completing their legal education. One study found a significant negative relationship between depression and academic performance.[49] Also, those with substance abuse issues tend to have lower grades.[50] Interestingly, some mental disorders, including anxiety and neuroticism, are correlated with higher grades.[51]

CONCLUSION

Mental toughness is many things and rather difficult to explain.
Its qualities are sacrifice and self-denial. Also, most importantly,
it is combined with a perfectly disciplined will that
refuses to give in.

VINCE LOMBARDI

Whether you are about to start or are in law school, you now have a better sense of what it takes to succeed. Practicing law is hard, so it should come as no surprise that law school is equally challenging. This means learning new study skills, writing unfamiliar types of essays, spending less time with friends, becoming more disciplined, and spending hours each day reading legal material. Though difficult and grueling at times, at the journey's end your mind will be permanently changed. You will become a more critical thinker, having learned what it means to "think like a lawyer."

REFERENCES

1. Kayla Morehead et al., *Instructor and Student Knowledge of Study Strategies*. 24 Memory 257, 258 (2016).

2. Melissa Abdullah and Ng Lee Yen, Improving Self-Regulated Learning with Self-Management Tool: An Empirical Study. Penerbit USM, Section 1.1 (2014).

3. Guy R. Loftman, *Study Habits and Their Effectiveness in Legal Education*, Journal of Legal Education, Vol. 27, p. 418 (1975).

4. Catherine Martin Christopher, *Normalizing Struggle*, 73 Arkansas Law Review 27, 36 (2020).

5. Professor Charles Kingsfield is a fictional law school professor at Harvard Law School. The Paper Chase, 1973.

6. Marissa K. Hartwig and John Dunlosky, *Study Strategies of College Students: Are Self-Testing and Scheduling Related to Achievement?* Psychonomic Bulletin Review, 19: 132 (2012).

7. Ibid.

8. Philip S. Babcock and Mindy Marks, *The Falling Time Cost of College: Evidence from Half a Century of Time Use Data* (2010).

9. Sean H. K. Kang, *Spaced Repetition Promotes Efficient and Effective Learning: Policy Implications for Instruction*. Instructional Strategies (2016). Vol. 3(1) 12–19.

10. Dorothy L. Worden, *Finding Process in Product: Prewriting and Revision in Timed Essay Responses*. Assessing Writing, Volume 14, Issue 3, 2009, Pages 157–177.

11. Gruneberg, Michael M.; Gruneberg, Michael; Morris, Peter Edwin. Theoretical Aspects of Memory (1994).

12. Mark McDaniel, Janis Anderson, Mary Derbish, and Nova Morrisette, *Testing*

the Testing Effect in the Classroom, European Journal of Cognitive Psychology, 494–513 (2007).

13. Jennifer Cooper and Regan Gurung, *Smarter Law Study Habits: An Empirical Analysis of Law Learning Strategies and Relationship with Law GPA*. 62 St. Louis University Law Journal 361 (Winter, 2018).

14. Ibid.

15. Professor Charles Kingsfield is a fictional law school professor at Harvard Law School in the movie The Paper Chase, 1973.

16. Henry L. Roediger III and Andrew C. Butler, *The Critical Role of Retrieval Practice in Long-Term Retention*. Trends in Cognitive Sciences, January 2011, Vol. 15, No. 1.

17. Bruce K. Britton and Abraham Tesser, *Effects of Time-Management Practices on College Grades*, Journal of Educational Psychology, Vol. 83, No. 3, 405–410 (1991).

18. Anastasiya Lipnevich and Jeffrey K. Smith, *Effects of Differential Feedback on Students' Examination Performance*, Journal of Experimental Psychology: Applied, Vol. 15, No. 4, 319–333 (2009).

19. Id. at 329.

20. S. H. McIntyre and J. M. Munson, *Exploring Cramming: Student Behaviors, Beliefs, and Learning Retention in the Principles of Marketing Course.* Journal of Marketing Education, 30(3):226–243 (2008).

21. Ben D. Wood, *Measurement of Law School Work*, Columbia Law Review, March 1924. *Measurement of Law School Work: II*, Columbia Law Review, March 1925. *Measurement of Law School Work: III*, Columbia Law Review, November 1927.

22. Patrick R. Krill, Ryan Johnson, and Linda Albert, *The Prevalence of Substance Use and Other Mental Health Concerns Among American Attorneys.* Journal of Addiction Medicine: January/February 2016 - Volume 10 - Issue 1 - p 46–52.

23. American Bar Association National Task Force on Lawyer Well-Being, *Creating a Movement to Improve Well-Being in the Legal Profession*, August 14, 2017.

    https://www.americanbar.org/content/dam/aba/images/abanews/ThePathToLawyerWellBeingReportRevFINAL.pdf Last retrieved on 8/9/21.

24. Alapin, Fichten, Libman, Creti, Bailes, and Wright, *How is Good and Poor Sleep in Older Adults and College Students Related to Daytime Sleepiness,*

Fatigue, and ability to Concentrate. Journal of Psychosomatic Research 49 (2000) 381–390.

25. The Pomodoro Technique, Francesco Cirillo (2007). http://baomee.info/pdf/technique/1.pdf Last retrieved on 11/13/20.

26. Emily Hunter and Cindy Wu, *Give Me a Better Break: Choosing Workday Break Activities to Maximize Resource Recovery.* Journal of Applied Psychology, pages 1–2 (2015).

27. Hunter and Wu, page 8.

28. Sanghoon Kang and Terri R. Kurtzberg, *Reach for your Cell Phone at your own Risk: The Cognitive Costs of Media Choice for Breaks.* Journal of Behavioral Addictions, pp. 395–403 (2019).

29. Fictional character in the movie Legally Blonde.

30. Roberto Assagioli, The Act of the Will, p. 47. Viking Press (1973).

31. Assagioli at p. 46.

32. Assagioli at p. 36.

33. Williams James, Talk to Teachers on Psychology, pp. 75–56. Holt (1925).

34. E. Boyd Barrett, Strength of Will and How to Develop It. Harper (1931).

35. Ibid.

36. Plato's Republic, Book 3, 411e.

37. John Ratey, Spark: The Revolutionary New Science of Exercise and the Brain. (2013).

38. Mickey T. Trockel, Michael D. Barnes, and Dennis L. Egget, *Health-Related Variables and Academic Performance Among First-Year College Students: Implications for Sleep and Other Behaviors,* Journal of American College Health, vol. 49 (November 2000).

39. Jack K. Trammell, *The Impact of Academic Accommodations on Final Grades in a Postsecondary Setting,* Journal of College Reading and Learning, 34 (Fall 2003).

40. Alcoholic Anonymous twelve steps:

    1. We admitted we were powerless over alcohol—that our lives had become unmanageable.

    2. Came to believe that a Power greater than ourselves could restore us to sanity.

3. Made a decision to turn our will and our lives over to the care of God as we understood Him.

4. Made a searching and fearless moral inventory of ourselves.

5. Admitted to God, to ourselves, and to another human being the exact nature of our wrongs.

6. Were entirely ready to have God remove all these defects of character.

7. Humbly asked Him to remove our shortcomings.

8. Made a list of all persons we had harmed, and became willing to make amends to them all.

9. Made direct amends to such people wherever possible, except when to do so would injure them or others.

10. Continued to take personal inventory and when we were wrong promptly admitted it.

11. Sought through prayer and meditation to improve our conscious contact with God, as we understood Him, praying only for knowledge of His will for us and the power to carry that out.

12. Having had a spiritual awakening as the result of these Steps, we tried to carry this message to alcoholics, and to practice these principles in all our affairs.

41. Alcoholics Anonymous website: https://www.aa.org/pages/en_US/what-is-aa (Last retrieved on 11/7/20).

42. Celebrate Recovery website: https://www.celebraterecovery.com/ (Last retrieved on 11/7/20).

43. Co-Dependents Anonymous website: https://coda.org/newcomers/ (Last retrieved on 11/7/20).

44. Food Addicts in Recovery Anonymous website: https://www.foodaddicts.org/what-is-fa (Last retrieved on 11/7/20).

45. Gamblers Anonymous website: http://www.gamblersanonymous.org/ga/node/1 (Last retrieved on 11/7/20).

46. Sex Addicts Anonymous website: https://saa-recovery.org/our-program/ (Last retrieved on 11/7/20).

47. Workaholics Anonymous website: https://www.workaholics-anonymous.org/ (Last retrieved on 11/7/20).

48. American Counseling Association website: https://www.counseling.org/ aca-community/learn-about-counseling/what-is-counseling (Last retrieved on 6/30/21).

49. Virginia Deroma, John Leach, and Patrick Leverett, The Relationship Between Depression and College Academic Performance, College Student Journal, vol. 43, issue 2, 325-334 (June 2009).

50. Soren Svanum and Zanita Zody, Psychopathology and College Grades, Journal of Counseling Psychology, Vol. 24, No. 1, 72–76 (2001).

51. Ibid.

APPENDIX 1: CASES

GARRATT V. DAILEY

Supreme Court of Washington (1955)

Brian Dailey (age five years, nine months) was visiting with Naomi Garratt, an adult and a sister of the plaintiff, Ruth Garratt, likewise an adult, in the back yard of the plaintiff's home, on July 16, 1951. It is plaintiff's contention that she came out into the back yard to talk with Naomi and that, as she started to sit down in a wood and canvas lawn chair, Brian deliberately pulled it out from under her. The only one of the three persons present so testifying was Naomi Garratt. (Ruth Garratt, the plaintiff, did not testify as to how or why she fell.) The trial court, unwilling to accept this testimony, adopted instead Brian Dailey's version of what happened, and made the following findings: that while Naomi Garratt and Brian Dailey were in the back yard the plaintiff, Ruth Garratt, came out of her house into the back yard. Sometime subsequent thereto defendant, Brian Dailey, picked up a lightly built wood and canvas lawn chair which was then and there located in the back yard of the above described premises, moved it sideways a few feet and seated himself therein, at which time he discovered the plaintiff, Ruth Garratt, about to sit down at the place where the lawn chair had formerly been, at which time he hurriedly got up from the chair and attempted to move it toward Ruth Garratt to aid her in sitting down in the chair; that due to the defendant's small size and lack of dexterity he was unable to get the lawn chair under the plaintiff in time to prevent her from falling to the ground. That plaintiff fell to the ground and sustained a fracture of her hip, and other injuries and damages as hereinafter set forth.

The preponderance of the evidence in this case establishes that when the defendant, Brian Dailey, moved the chair in question he did not have any willful or unlawful purpose in doing so; that he did not have any intent to injure the plaintiff, or any intent to bring about any unauthorized or offensive contact with her person or any objects appurtenant thereto; that the circumstances which immediately preceded the fall of the plaintiff established that the defendant, Brian Dailey, did not have purpose, intent or design to perform a prank or to effect an assault and battery upon the person of the plaintiff.

In our analysis of the applicable law, we start with the basic premise that Brian, whether five or fifty-five, must have committed some wrongful act before he could be liable for appellant's injuries. It is urged that Brian's action in moving the chair constituted a battery.

A definition (not all-inclusive but sufficient for our purpose) of a battery is the intentional infliction of a harmful bodily contact upon another. In order that an act may be done with the intention of bringing about a harmful or offensive contact or an apprehension thereof to a particular person, either the other or a third person, the act must be done for the purpose of causing the contact or apprehension or with knowledge on the part of the actor that such contact or apprehension is substantially certain to be produced.

We have here the conceded volitional act of Brian, i.e., the moving of a chair. Had the plaintiff proved to the satisfaction of the trial court that Brian moved the chair while she was in the act of sitting down, Brian's action would patently have been for the purpose or with the intent of causing the plaintiff's bodily contact with the ground, and she would be entitled to a judgment against him for the resulting damages.

A battery would be established if, in addition to plaintiff's fall, it was proved that, when Brian moved the chair, he knew with substantial certainty that the plaintiff would attempt to sit down where the chair had been. Without such knowledge, there would be nothing wrongful about Brian's act in moving the chair and, there being no wrongful act, there would be no liability.

While a finding that Brian had no such knowledge can be inferred from the findings made, we believe that before the plaintiff's action in such a case should be dismissed there should be no question but that the trial court had passed upon that issue; hence, the case should be remanded for clarification of the findings to specifically cover the question of Brian's knowledge, because intent could be inferred therefrom. If the court finds that he had such knowledge the necessary intent will be established and the plaintiff will be entitled to recover, even though there was no purpose to injure or embarrass the plaintiff. If Brian did not have such knowledge, there was no wrongful act by him and the basic premise of liability on the theory of a battery was not established.

COHEN V. SMITH

Appellate Court of Illinois (1995)

Patricia Cohen was admitted to St. Joseph Memorial Hospital ("Hospital") to deliver her baby. After an examination, Cohen was informed that it would be necessary for her to have a cesarean section. Cohen and her husband allegedly informed her physician, who in turn advised the Hospital staff, that the couple's religious beliefs prohibited Cohen from being seen unclothed by a male. Cohen's doctor assured her husband that their religious convictions would be respected.

During Cohen's cesarean section, Roger Smith, a male nurse on staff at the Hospital, allegedly observed and touched Cohen's naked body. Cohen and her husband filed suit against Nurse Smith and the Hospital. The trial court allowed defendants' motions to dismiss. We reverse.

Historically, battery was first and foremost a systematic substitution for private retribution. Protecting personal integrity has always been viewed as an important basis for battery. Consequently, the defendant is liable not only for contacts which do actual physical harm, but also for those relatively trivial ones which are merely offensive and insulting. This application of battery to remedy offensive and insulting conduct is deeply ingrained in our legal history. As early as 1784, a Pennsylvania defendant was prosecuted for striking the cane of a French ambassador. The court furthered the distinction between harmful offensive batteries and non-harmful offensive batteries:

"As to the assault, this is, perhaps, one of that kind, in which the insult is more to be considered than the actual damage; for, though no great bodily pain is suffered by a blow on the palm of the hand, or the skirt of the coat, yet these are clearly within the definition of assault and battery, and among gentlemen too often induce dueling and terminate in murder." Respublica v. De Longchamps (Pa.1784).

Causing actual physical harm is not an element of battery. A plaintiff is entitled to demand that the defendant refrain from the offensive touching, although the contact results in no visible injury.

According to the complaint, despite being informed of Cohen's religious beliefs, Nurse Smith, an agent and employee of the Hospital, intentionally saw and touched Cohen's naked body.

The allegation that both Nurse Smith and the Hospital were informed in advance of plaintiffs' religious beliefs is important in this case, because the religious convictions of plaintiffs might not be those of most people who enter the hospital to give birth. As a matter of fact, plaintiffs' counsel candidly conceded that there would be no cause of action for battery if Patricia Cohen had been placed in Nurse Smith's and the Hospital's care in an emergency situation in which Patricia had been unable to inform the Hospital or its agents of her beliefs. Plaintiffs' attorney acknowledged that his clients' moral and religious views are not widely held in the community and, because of this, plaintiffs could state a claim against defendants only if the plaintiffs plead that the defendants had knowledge of those beliefs. Specifically, plaintiffs contend that defendants' knowledge is clearly illustrated by an allegation in the plaintiffs' amended complaint that Nurse Smith requested the presence of the Murphysboro City Police at the Hospital to prevent Mr. Cohen from objecting to Nurse Smith's presence in the operating room while Mrs. Cohen was naked, and to physically restrain Mr. Cohen if necessary.

The fact that the plaintiffs hold deeply ingrained religious beliefs which are not shared by the majority of society does not mean that those beliefs deserve less protection than more mainstream religious beliefs. The plaintiffs were not trying to force their religion on other people; they were only insisting that their beliefs be respected by the Hospital and the Hospital staff.

When she informed the Hospital of her moral and religious beliefs against being viewed and touched by males, the Hospital was free to refuse to accede to those demands. But, according to her complaint, when Cohen made her wishes known to the Hospital, it, at least implicitly, agreed to provide her with treatment within the restrictions placed by her beliefs.

Although most people in modern society have come to accept the necessity of being seen unclothed and being touched by members of the opposite sex during medical treatment, the plaintiffs had not accepted these procedures and, according to their complaint, had informed defendants of their convictions. This case is similar to cases involving Jehovah's Witnesses who were unwilling to accept blood transfusions because of religious convictions. Although most people do not share the Jehovah's Witnesses' beliefs about blood transfusions, our society, and our courts, accept their right to have that belief. Similarly, the courts have consistently recognized individuals' rights to refuse medical treatment even if such a refusal would result in an increased likelihood of the individual's death.

A person's right to refuse or accept medical care is not one to be interfered with lightly. As Justice Cardozo stated, "Every human being of adult years and sound mind has a right to determine what shall be done with his own body; and a surgeon who performs an operation without his patient's consent commits an assault, for which he is liable in damages."

Knowing interference with the right of determination is battery. Accepting as true the plaintiffs allegations that they informed defendants of their religious beliefs and that defendants persisted in treating Patricia Cohen as they would have treated a patient without those beliefs, we conclude that the trial court erred in dismissing the battery count.

BASKA V. SCHERZER

Supreme Court of Kansas (2007)

Baska had given her daughter Ashley, a high school senior, permission to organize a scavenger hunt with some friends. When people returned, a number of them remained at the Baskas' home for a party. Scherzer and Madrigal were both at the party. Around midnight, an altercation broke out between Scherzer and Madrigal. Madrigal approached Scherzer from behind, and the two boys began to push each other and throw punches at one another. Upon being informed of the fight by one of her daughter's friends, Baska yelled at the boys to stop in order to break up the fight. When they continued to fight, Baska placed herself between the boys and was punched in the face, losing several teeth and receiving injuries to her neck and jaw. Baska is certain that Scherzer hit her in the face; she also believes that Madrigal punched her in the back of the head.

The Restatement (Second) of Torts and this court's decisions discuss this situation as being contemplated by the long-standing doctrine of transferred intent. The Restatement explains that the term intent, as it is used in the law of torts, denotes that the actor desires to cause the consequences of his act, or that he believes that the consequences are substantially certain to result from it. Intent is not, however, limited to consequences which are desired. If the actor knows that the consequences are certain, or substantially certain, to result from his act, and still goes ahead, he is treated by the law as if he had in fact desired to produce the result. However, an action need not be directed at the plaintiff in order to give rise to liability for intentional torts. Rather, the doctrine of transferred intent states that the tort of battery may be committed, although the person struck or hit by the defendant is not the one whom he intended to strike or hit. It is enough that the actor intends to produce such an effect upon some other person and that his act so intended is the legal cause of a harmful contact to the other. It is not necessary that the actor know or have reason even to suspect that the other is in the vicinity of the third person whom the actor intends to affect and, therefore, that he should recognize that his act, though directed against the third person, involves a risk of causing bodily harm to the other so that the act would be negligent toward him.

Defendants Madrigal and Scherzer intended to punch someone (the other defendant) and did punch someone (the plaintiff). Although their actions were not specifically directed at the plaintiff, their punches were intentional acts and did injure Baska. If defendant unlawfully aims at one person and hits another, under the doctrine of transferred intent he is guilty of battery on the person hit, the injury being the direct, natural, and probable consequence of the wrongful act. So, if one of two persons fighting unintentionally strikes a third, the person so striking is liable in an action by the third person for a battery.

PALSGRAF V. LONG ISLAND RAILROAD

Court of Appeals of New York (1928)

CARDOZO, C. J.

Plaintiff was standing on a platform of defendant's railroad after buying a ticket to go to Rockaway Beach. A train stopped at the station, bound for another place. Two men ran forward to catch it. One of the men reached the platform of the car without mishap, though the train was already moving. The other man, carrying a package, jumped aboard the car, but seemed unsteady as if about to fall. A guard on the car, who had held the door open, reached forward to help him in, and another guard on the platform pushed him from behind. In this act, the package was dislodged, and fell upon the rails. It was a package of small size, about fifteen inches long, and was covered by a newspaper. In fact it contained fireworks, but there was nothing in its appearance to give notice of its contents. The fireworks when they fell exploded. The shock of the explosion threw down some scales at the other end of the platform many feet away. The scales struck the plaintiff, causing injuries for which she sues.

The conduct of the defendant's guard, if a wrong in its relation to the holder of the package, was not a wrong in its relation to the plaintiff, standing far away. Relatively to her it was not negligence at all. Nothing in the situation gave notice that the falling package had in it the potency of peril to persons thus removed. Negligence is not actionable unless it involves the invasion of a legally protected interest, the violation of a right. Proof of negligence in the air, so to speak, will not do. Negligence is the absence of care, according to the circumstances. The plaintiff, as she stood upon the platform of the station, might claim to be protected against intentional invasion of her bodily security. Such invasion is not charged. She might claim to be protected against unintentional invasion by conduct involving in the thought of reasonable men an unreasonable hazard that such invasion would ensue. If no hazard was apparent to the eye of ordinary vigilance, an act innocent and harmless, at least to outward seeming, with reference to her, did not take to itself the quality of a tort because it happened to be a wrong, though apparently not one involving the risk of bodily insecurity, with reference to someone else. In every instance, before negligence can be predicated of a given act, back of the act must be sought and found a duty to the individual complaining, the observance of which would have averted or avoided the injury.

A different conclusion will involve us, and swiftly too, in a maze of contradictions. A guard stumbles over a package which has been left upon a platform. It seems to be a bundle of newspapers. It turns out to be a can of dynamite. To the eye of ordinary vigilance, the bundle is abandoned waste, which may be kicked or trod on with impunity. Is a passenger at the other end of the platform protected by the law against the unsuspected hazard concealed beneath the waste? If not, is the result to be any different, so far as the distant passenger is concerned, when the guard stumbles over a valise which a truckman or a porter has left upon the walk? The passenger far away, if the victim of a wrong at all, has a cause of action, not derivative, but original and primary. His claim to be protected against invasion of his bodily security is neither greater nor less because the act resulting in the invasion is a wrong to another far removed. In this case, the rights that are said to have been violated, are not even of the same order. The man was not injured in his person nor even put in danger. The purpose of the act, as well as its effect, was to make his person safe. It there was a wrong to him at all, which may very well be doubted it was a wrong to a property interest only, the safety of his package. Out of this wrong to property, which threatened injury to nothing else, there has passed, we are told, to the plaintiff by derivation or succession a right of action for the invasion of an interest of another order, the right to bodily security. The diversity of interests emphasizes the futility of the effort to build the plaintiff's right upon the basis of a wrong to someone else.

The argument for the plaintiff is built upon the shifting meanings of such words as *wrong* and *wrongful*, and shares their instability. What the plaintiff must show is "a wrong" to herself; i.e., a violation of her own right, and not merely a wrong to someone else, nor conduct "wrongful" because unsocial, but not "a wrong" to anyone. We are told that one who drives at reckless speed through a crowded city street is guilty of a negligent act and therefore of a wrongful one, irrespective of the consequences. Negligent the act is, and wrongful in the sense that it is unsocial, but wrongful and unsocial in relation to other travelers, only because the eye of vigilance perceives the risk of damage. If the same act were to be committed on a speedway or a race course, it would lose its wrongful quality. The risk reasonably to be perceived defines the duty to be obeyed, and risk imports relation; it is risk to another or to others within the range of apprehension. This does not mean, of course, that one who launches a destructive force is always relieved of liability, if the force, though known to be destructive, pursues an unexpected path. "It was not necessary that the defendant should have had notice of the particular method in which an accident would occur, if the possibility of an accident was clear to the ordinarily prudent eye." Some acts, such as shooting are so imminently dangerous to anyone who may come within reach of the missile however unexpectedly, as to impose a duty of prevision not far from that of an insurer. Even today, and much oftener in earlier stages of the law, one acts sometimes at one's peril. These cases aside, wrong is defined in terms of the natural or probable, at least when unintentional. The range of reasonable apprehension is at times a question for the court, and at times, if varying inferences are possible, a question for the jury. Here, by concession, there was nothing in the situation to suggest to the most cautious mind that the parcel wrapped in newspaper would spread wreckage through the station. If the guard had thrown it down knowingly and willfully, he would not have threatened the plaintiff's safety, so far as appearances could warn him. His conduct would not have involved, even then, an unreasonable probability of invasion of her bodily security. Liability can be no greater where the act is inadvertent.

The law of causation, remote or proximate, is thus foreign to the case before us. The question of liability is always anterior to the question of the measure of the consequences that go with liability. If there is no tort to be redressed, there is no occasion to consider what damage might be recovered if there were a finding of a tort.

ANDREWS, J. (dissenting)

Assisting a passenger to board a train, the defendant's servant negligently knocked a package from his arms. It fell between the platform and the cars. Of its contents the servant knew and could know nothing. A violent explosion followed. The concussion broke some scales standing a considerable distance away. In falling, they injured the plaintiff, an intending passenger.

Upon these facts, may she recover the damages she has suffered in an action brought against the master? The result we shall reach depends upon our theory as to the nature of negligence. Is it a relative concept— the breach of some duty owing to a particular person or to particular persons? Or, where there is an act which unreasonably threatens the safety of others, is the doer liable for all its proximate consequences, even where they result in injury to one who would generally be thought to be outside the radius of danger? This is not a mere dispute as to words. We might not believe that to the average mind the dropping of the bundle would seem to involve the probability of harm to the plaintiff standing many feet away whatever might be the case as to the owner or to one so near as to be likely to be struck by its fall. If, however, we adopt the second hypothesis, we have to inquire only as to the relation between cause and effect. We deal in terms of proximate cause, not of negligence.

Negligence may be defined roughly as an act or omission which unreasonably does or may affect the rights of others, or which unreasonably fails to protect one's self from the dangers resulting from such acts. Here I confine myself to the first branch of the definition. Nor do I comment on the word *unreasonable*. For present purposes it sufficiently describes that average of conduct that society requires of its members.

But we are told that "there is no negligence unless there is in the particular case a legal duty to take care, and this duty must be one which is owed to the plaintiff himself and not merely to others." This I think too narrow a conception. Where there is the unreasonable act, and some right that may be affected there is negligence whether damage does or does not result. That is immaterial. Should we drive down Broadway at a reckless speed, we are negligent whether we strike an approaching car or miss it by an inch. The act itself is wrongful. It is a wrong not only to those who happen to be within the radius of danger, but to all who might have been there—a wrong to the public at large. Such is the language of the street. Such again and again their language in speaking of the duty of some defendant and discussing proximate cause in cases where such a discussion is wholly irrelevant on any other theory. As was said by Mr. Justice Holmes many years ago:

"The measure of the defendant's duty in determining whether a wrong has been committed is one thing, the measure of liability when a wrong has been committed is another."

Due care is a duty imposed on each one of us to protect society from unnecessary danger, not to protect A, B, or C alone.

It may well be that there is no such thing as negligence in the abstract. "Proof of negligence in the air, so to speak, will not do." In an empty world negligence would not exist. It does involve a relationship between man and his fellows, but not merely a relationship between man and those whom he might reasonably expect his act would injure; rather, a relationship between him and those whom he does in fact injure. If his act has a tendency to harm someone, it harms him a mile away as surely as it does those on the scene.

The proposition is this: Every one owes to the world at large the duty of refraining from those acts that may unreasonably threaten the safety of others. Such an act occurs. Not only is he wronged to whom harm, might reasonably be expected to result, but he also who is in fact injured, even if he be outside what would generally be thought the danger zone. There needs be duty due the one complaining, but this is not a duty to a particular individual because as to him harm might be expected. Harm to someone being the natural result of the act, not only that one alone, but all those in fact injured may complain. We have never, I think, held otherwise. Unreasonable risk being taken, its consequences are not confined to those who might probably be hurt.

The right to recover damages rests on additional considerations. The plaintiff's rights must be injured, and this injury must be caused by the negligence. We build a dam but are negligent as to its foundations. Breaking, it injures property downstream. We are not liable if all this happened because of some reason other than the insecure foundation. But, when injuries do result from out unlawful act, we are liable for the consequences. It does not matter that they are unusual, unexpected, unforeseen, and unforeseeable. But there is one limitation. The damages must be so connected with the negligence that the latter may be said to be the proximate cause of the former.

These two words have never been given an inclusive definition. What is a cause in a legal sense, still more what is a proximate cause, depend in each case upon many considerations, as does the existence of negligence itself. Any philosophical doctrine of causation does not help us. A boy throws a stone into a pond. The ripples spread. The water level rises. The history of that pond is altered to all eternity. It will be altered by other causes also. Yet it will be forever the resultant of all causes combined. Each one will have an influence. How great only omniscience can say. You may speak of a chain, or, if you please, a net. An analogy is of little aid. Each cause brings about future events. Without each the future would not be the same. Each is proximate in the sense it is essential. But that is not what we mean by the word. Nor on the other hand do we mean sole cause. There is no such thing.

A cause, but not the proximate cause. What we do mean by the word *proximate* is that, because of convenience, of public policy, of a rough sense of justice, the law arbitrarily declines to trace a series of events beyond a certain point. This is not logic. It is practical politics. We may regret that the line was drawn just where it was, but drawn somewhere it had to be. Cause it surely was. The words we used were simply indicative of our notions of public policy. Other courts think differently. But somewhere they reach the point where they cannot say the stream comes from any one source.

There are no fixed rules to govern our judgment. There are simply matters of which we may take account. We have in a somewhat different connection spoken of "the stream of events." We have asked whether that stream was deflected—whether it was forced into new and unexpected channels. This is rather rhetoric than law. There is in truth little to guide us other than common sense.

The act upon which defendant's liability rests is knocking an apparently harmless package onto the platform. The act was negligent. For its proximate consequences the defendant is liable. If its contents were broken, to the owner; if it fell upon and crushed a passenger's foot, then to him; if it exploded and injured one in the immediate vicinity, to him also as to A in the illustration. Mrs. Palsgraf was standing some distance away. How far cannot be told from the record—apparently 25 or 30 feet, perhaps less. Except for the explosion, she would not have been injured. We are told by the appellant in his brief, "It cannot be denied that the explosion was the direct cause of the plaintiff's injuries." So it was a substantial factor in producing the result—there was here a natural and continuous sequence—direct connection. The only intervening cause was that, instead of blowing her to the ground, the concussion smashed the weighing machine which in turn fell upon her. There was no remoteness in time, little in space. And surely, given such an explosion as here, it needed no great foresight to predict that the natural result would be to injure one on the platform at no greater distance from its scene than was the plaintiff. Just how no one might be able to predict. Whether by flying fragments, by broken glass, by wreckage of machines or structures no one could say. But injury in some form was most probable.

Under these circumstances I cannot say as a matter of law that the plaintiff's injuries were not the proximate result of the negligence.

APPENDIX 2: CASE BRIEFS

GARRATT V. DAILEY

Facts: Five-year-old boy moved chair from where it was normally kept, resulting in Garratt falling down when she tried to sit.

Issue: Whether Dailey had the intent to commit a battery by moving the chair that Garratt was going to sit on.

Rule: The intent to commit a battery is present when the defendant knew to a substantial certainty that the contact would occur.

Application: Brian was in Ruth Garratt's backyard when he moved a lawn chair a few feet and then sat in the chair. When he saw that Ruth Garratt was about to sit in the spot where the chair had been located, he tried to move it back. But he could not get it back in time to prevent her from falling. When Brian initially moved the chair, he did not know that Ruth Garratt would go back to the spot where the chair had been and then sit down in that spot even though the chair had been moved.

Conclusion: Brian did not have the intent to commit a battery because he did not know to a substantial certainty that his act would result in Ruth Garratt falling down.

COHEN V. SMITH

Facts: Cohen (religious) had baby in hospital, where male nurse saw her naked.

Issue: Whether contact by Smith in a hospital room was a battery when Cohen informed Smith that she did not want to be touched by him.

Rule: Battery occurs when a plaintiff demands that the defendant refrain from an offensive touching, even when there is no visible injury.

Application: Cohen had religious beliefs that did not allow her to be seen naked or touched by men other than her husband. Before she entered a hospital to have a baby, she informed the hospital of her beliefs, and they agreed to respect her wishes. Smith was a male nurse at the hospital, who saw and touched Cohen against her wishes. Though Cohen was not physically harmed by Smith's contact, his contact was highly offensive to her because the contact violated Cohen's deeply held religious beliefs.

Conclusion: Smith committed a battery because he contacted Cohen after he consented not to touch her.

BASKA V. SCHERZER

Facts: Mom gets between two fighting boys and gets punched.

Issue: Whether defendant's intent to commit a battery directed at one person can transfer to an unintended victim.

Rule: When defendant desires and attempts to hit one person, he is guilty of battery when he hits a different person.

Application: Two teenagers began fighting, and Baska moved between them to stop the fight. The boys did not immediately realize that Baska was between them, so they kept intentionally swinging at each other but accidentally hit Baska.

Conclusion: The boys committed a battery because their intent to hit each other transferred to Baska.

PALSGRAF V. LONG ISLAND RAILROAD

Facts: Palsgraf was sitting at railway station. Railroad employees were negligent in helping different passengers onto the moving train, resulting in unmarked package that one passenger was carrying to fall on the tracks. The package happened to contain fireworks, resulting in explosion. Scales near Palsgraf fell on her.

Issue: Did the railroad owe a duty of care to the plaintiff when the defendant's negligence was directed towards someone else?

Rule: There is no duty owed to a plaintiff when the defendant could not have reasonably foreseen the risk of their negligent act.

Analysis: Two railroad employees helped a passenger board a moving train, which was unreasonable. The employees saw a package in the arms of the passenger, which was dislodged and fell onto the tracks, resulting in an explosion. The explosion caused some scales to fall down on Mrs. Palsgraf. However, the employees had no reason to believe the package contained explosives. At most, the only foreseeable consequence of helping the men boarding a train is that they would fall down, or that whatever they were carrying would be damaged. Also, Mrs. Palsgraf was not even near the spot where the package fell onto the tracks.

Conclusion: Palsgraf was not a foreseeable plaintiff because the defendants could not have reasonably foreseen that she would be injured by exploding fireworks.

Dissent: A duty of care is owed to everyone when the conduct was unreasonable. The second issue is whether the defendant was the proximate cause of the injury.

APPENDIX 3:
SAMPLE EXAMS

TORTS MIDTERM ESSAY EXAM

Rick lives in DeKalb and wants some fresh sweet corn. He wants some because his dying grandmother, who might not make it through the night, has asked him for "one last bite of sweet corn" before she dies. After going to Fatty's Pub & Grille for a few drinks, Rick leaves at 2 am and finds a nearby corn field, which happens to be owned by Sarah and leased to and farmed by Sean. After parking his car on the public road, Rick enters the field and starts looking for some delicious-looking corn. While looking around, Rick sees a barn and is curious as to what is inside the barn. Just as he is about to enter the barn, Rick hears a sound from inside the barn that scares him. As Rick turns to run away, he accidentally bumps the barn door, causing the door to close and lock.

Inside the barn was Sean, who was taking care of some animals. When Sean heard the door close, he went to the door, found that it was locked, and realized he was now trapped inside the barn. After two or three minutes, Sean remembered that some hay had been delivered the day before and was in a giant pile below the second-story window, about 30 feet off the ground. So Sean went up the ladder to the second story, jumped out the window, and landed safely on the pile of hay. The government has chosen to not file any criminal charges against Rick.

Discuss all tort issues reasonably raised by this fact pattern. Do NOT discuss any potential affirmative defenses or negligence.

TORTS FINAL ANALYTICAL
(BAR STYLE) EXAM

Jackie Oldham, who is 82 years old, owns a home with a basement apartment. Jackie lives on the top level of the home, and she rents the basement apartment to Pablo. Before Pablo moves into the basement apartment, Jackie makes numerous repairs. One repair in the basement apartment involves new windows. Jackie notices some dry-rot around the windows, but instead of fixing it she paints over the dry-rot. A few months after Pablo moves in, Druggie decides to break into the basement apartment to steal things. As he is breaking through one of the windows, the window gives way, resulting in Druggie being injured by broken glass. A police investigation establishes that the dry-rot is responsible for the window giving way.

While in jail awaiting trial, Druggie discovers what Jackie has done. He has access to the Internet, so he writes the following on his Twitter feed: "Jackie Oldham is an old immoral hag—she probably has dozens of cats." Jackie's friends see the post and tell her about it, and at least one friend uninvites Jackie to a party because of the tweet. Jackie, who does not own any cats, is very embarrassed and ashamed by Druggie's tweet.

Discuss all issues reasonably raised in a lawsuit by Druggie for his injuries. Also, discuss all issues reasonably raised in a Defamation action by Jackie against Druggie.

TORTS FINAL ISSUE SPOTTER ESSAY EXAM

The State of North Carolina, concerned with roller skating rink safety, enacted statute 99E-11. Below is the full statute, which does not refer to any other section of the State Code:

The roller skating rink operator, to the extent practicable, shall:

(1) When the rink is open for sessions, have at least one floor guard on duty for approximately every 200 skaters.

(2) Maintain the skating surface in reasonably safe condition and clean and inspect the skating surface before each session.

(3) Check rental skates on a regular basis to ensure the skates are in good mechanical condition.

This statute shall not be construed to impose any criminal penalty or fine on violators of this provision.

Bill's Roller Skating Rink (BRSR) is located in Concord, NC (10 miles north of Charlotte, NC). Sarah wanted to learn how to skate, so she went to BRSR on a busy Saturday night when there were 420 people skating. BRSR had two floor guards on duty, though one of them was ill and often during skate sessions had to skate to the bathroom. Before each session Owner looked out his office window—adjacent to the rink—to see if there was anything on the rink. While looking down the 200 feet of rink from his chair, he would send someone to pick up anything he saw on the floor. Finally, BRSR inspected the rental skates every year on March 15 to ensure that the skates were in good mechanical condition.

Sarah rented her skates from BRSR and noticed that one of the wheels was a bit wobbly, but she was in a hurry to skate. While Sarah was skating, during a time when one of the floor guards was in the bathroom, something happened and she fell down—she was unconscious for 30 minutes and does not recall what happened just before the fall. A witness said that he saw Sarah suddenly lose control for a few seconds before falling on the concrete rink.

Because of a large bruise on her head Sarah was rushed to a Concord, NC, hospital, where she was examined by Dr. Kildare. Dr. Kildare told Sarah that there was no immediate danger, that the hospital did not have the equipment to do a thorough examination, and that the hospitals in Charlotte did have better equipment (the equipment in Charlotte can check for problems inside the skull electronically, without the need for surgery). Dr. Kildare recommended immediate minor surgery so that he could examine her bruised head. Dr. Kildare had read that in the 1940s doctors in the United States routinely made a small incision at the impact point and examined the tissue under the skin, which is what he did with Sarah. While examining the tissue under Sarah's skin he noticed signs of a brain tumor, so he immediately opened her skull—he did not find a tumor, but the incision left a permanent scar on Sarah's face. At trial, an expert for Dr. Kildare will testify it is common practice in the medical profession to open the skull when signs for brain tumors, like the one with Sarah, are found by a doctor.

Sarah's boyfriend, Peter, hearing about the accident drove to the hospital. Peter was driving west on Main Street when he came to a complete stop in a right-turn-only lane at a stop sign. In violation of state law, he failed to turn on his turn signal. Derik was driving at the posted speed limit, heading north on Elm Street. Derik's baby began to cry so he turned around for about one second to check on him. He turned back around just in time to see his car about to hit Peter's car, which was at a complete stop on Main Street. Derik swerved but hit Peter's car. Peter had some gardening supplies in the front seat and was cut on the arm during the accident, which introduced bacteria from the gardening supplies into his blood. Paramedic quickly arrived on the scene, cut his hands on the gardening tools, and became infected by the same bacteria.

Peter was rushed to the hospital, but the bacteria was immune to modern drugs, and Peter's arm was amputated. Paramedic also had a limb amputated. After the accident Peter had nightmares of cars hitting him, and he developed bleeding stomach ulcers.

Around 10:00 p.m. that night Derik wanted free beer, so he placed a mouse in a beer bottle and took it to Beer Company. He parked in a "visitor" spot and went to the "Visitor Entrance." A sign said: "Visitors must ring the bell and wait for someone to let them in." However, Derik noticed that the door had not been closed tightly, so he opened the door and entered. After a confrontation with Night Manager he accidently wandered into a locked room. About an hour later Night Manager showed up and told him to get off a bag of hops he was sleeping on. Unknown to Derik there was a sharp guillotine device nearby that was used to open the bags quickly. Derik jumped toward the guillotine device, which caused it to come down and amputate his right foot.

Fully discuss all issues reasonably raised by this fact pattern. Do not discuss Intentional Torts.

TORTS MIDTERM ISSUE SPOTTER ESSAY EXAM

Timed exercise: 60 minutes. CLOSED book and NO NOTES

John went to a local store owned and operated by Frank. While shopping inside the store, John saw Sandy, a former girlfriend he had broken up with a few years earlier. Sandy hated John for the breakup and for years was planning her revenge. Sandy walked to the back of the store to the meat department, where she found an old knife owned by the store. She decided, as her revenge, it would be funny to scare John. So with knife in hand, she walked quietly behind him, raised the knife, and planned to scream. Before she could scream, he suddenly turned around and hit the knife with his face, leaving a nasty large gash on his cheek. Startled, Sandy accidently dropped the knife, which broke in half when it hit the tile floor.

John was in pain, angry, and began yelling at Sandy. Frank heard the yelling and then saw the blood, so he told both of them to leave his store immediately. Sandy ran out of the store, but John said, "I will leave when I am good and ready." To help stop the massive bleeding, John walked over to the aisle where the store sold medical supplies, grabbed a box of bandages, and then placed a large bandage on his cheek, which stopped the bleeding.

John left the store without paying for the bandages and drove home, where he grabbed his gun. He drove to Sandy's apartment but didn't know Sandy had moved out over a year earlier—Matt was the new tenant in the apartment. John pounded on Matt's door, screaming, "I'm going to kill you when you open this door!" Matt lived on the top floor of a twelve-story building. There was one door into his apartment, though he owned a rope ladder that he had purchased for a possible fire emergency. He could attach it to a window and then very slowly get to the ground. John fired a few rounds through the door, with one bullet breaking a vase about a foot away from Matt. At that point Matt decided to use the rope ladder and escape from the apartment.

Neighbor heard the gunshots, grabbed a baseball bat, and ran outside to see what the commotion was about. When Neighbor saw John, he confronted him, asking him what he was doing. John said, "That's none of your business." Neighbor said, "It is my business, and if you don't like it, then why don't you shoot me?" John then shot Neighbor in the leg. As Neighbor was falling down, he took a swing at John, knocking him unconscious. After Neighbor ran out of his apartment, his Wife followed him and was standing about ten feet behind her husband. Wife saw John shoot Neighbor, her husband.

While Matt was slowly going down the rope ladder, Sarah saw Matt from her eighth-floor apartment. Believing Matt was a burglar, Sarah took some boiling water from the stove and dropped it on Matt. The scalding hot water hit Matt, and he fell to the ground, resulting in severe injuries.

Discuss all issues raised by these facts. Also, discuss possible affirmative defenses. Do not discuss Negligence.

TORTS POLICY QUESTION

The State legislature is considering legislation to abolish contributory negligence and replace it with pure comparative fault. Fully discuss the advantages and disadvantages of both systems, explaining why you believe one system is superior to the other.

APPENDIX 4: SAMPLE
EXAM ISSUE OUTLINES

TORTS MIDTERM ISSUE OUTLINE

Issue 1: Trespass to Land (40% of grade)

Rule Statement

- Intent to enter the land in possession of another.
- Intent is the desire or knowledge to a substantial certainty that you are entering land.
- Land includes the ground, what is below the ground, and above the ground. It also includes everything attached to the land.
- Possession of the land includes those who currently possess it, and those with a reversionary interest (i.e., the owner of the land).
- Actual harm is not required as nominal damages are available.
- Alcohol consumption does not negate the intent element.
- Entering the land occurs when one goes onto someone else's realty.

Application

RELEVANT FACTS

- The land was owned by Sarah and rented by Sean.
- Rick entered the land, looking for sweet corn for his mother.
- Rick bumps the barn door.
- Rick had been drinking alcohol at a bar before driving his car to the corn field.

LOGICAL CONCLUSIONS AND INFERENCES

- Both Sarah and Sean can bring a trespass to land action against Rick. Sarah, as the one with a reversionary interest, and Sean, as the current possessor of the land.

- Rick desired to enter the land, established by him parking his car next to the land, and then walking on the ground, looking to steal corn.
- Rick bumped the barn door. The barn is attached to the land, therefore it is included in the trespass.
- Even if Rick's judgment was clouded because of alcohol consumption, that does not change the fact that he intended to enter someone else's land.
- Rick is liable for trespass to land and nominal damages are available.

Issue 2: False Imprisonment (40% of grade)

Rule Statement

- False imprisonment occurs when a defendant unlawfully acts to intentionally cause confinement or restraint of the victim within a bounded area.
- Intent is when the defendant desires or knows to a substantial certainty that their action will confine the plaintiff.
- A person must be bounded in all directions.
- Confinement occurs when someone is restrained, and can occur through physical barriers.
- Confinement can occur for any amount of time, even very short amounts of time.
- If a person escapes by using heroic efforts, the law deems them to have still been confined.

Application

RELEVANT FACTS

- Rick accidently bumped the door, causing it to lock.
- Sean was in the barn when the door was locked, trapping him inside.
- After two minutes of being trapped, Sean recalled that he could climb a ladder to the second story window and jump 30

feet into a pile of hay.
- He made the jump safely.

LOGICAL CONCLUSIONS AND INFERENCES

- Rick did not desire to confine Sean—this was an accident. (See transferred intent below.)
- The barn counts as a bounded area because it had four walls and one second-story window.
- Though Sean was only confined for a few minutes, that is sufficient for False Imprisonment.
- Sean jumped 30 feet into a pile of hay, which is deemed a heroic effort. Therefore, the confinement element is met.
- Rick committed False Imprisonment.

Issue 3: Transferred Intent (20% of grade)

Rule Statement

- The transferred intent doctrine applies to battery, assault, false imprisonment, trespass to chattel, and trespass to land. If the defendant intends any of these five torts but his acts instead or in addition result in any of the other five, the defendant is liable even though he did not intend the other tort.

Application

RELEVANT FACTS

- Rick desired to enter the land rented by Sean, so he had the intent necessary for Trespass to Land.
- Rick did not have the intent to confine Sean—that was an accident.

LOGICAL CONCLUSIONS AND INFERENCES

- The intent to commit trespass to land transfers to the false imprisonment.

- Therefore, the intent element to false imprisonment is met through the transferred intent doctrine.

TORTS FINAL ANALYTICAL (BAR STYLE) ISSUE OUTLINE

Issue 1: Who owes a duty of care (owner or tenant) [20% of grade]

Rule Statement

- Landlords generally owe no duty to their tenants or those who enter the tenant's land. However, the duty shifts to the landlord when the landlord makes a negligent repair.

Analysis

RELEVANT FACTS

- Jackie is the landlord and rented the basement apartment to Pablo.
- Before Pablo moved in, Jackie made many repairs to the apartment. She noticed the dry-rot around the windows, but rather than fixing the damage she painted over the dry-rot.

LOGICAL CONCLUSIONS AND INFERENCES

- Jackie was negligent in failing to make the repair to the windows, therefore she will owe a duty to those who are injured by the negligent repair.

Issue 2: Negligence [20% of grade]

Rule Statement

- Status of the plaintiff: The status of the plaintiff on the land defines the duty owed to the plaintiff by the land possessor or landlord. When a plaintiff is not allowed on the property, then the plaintiff is called a trespasser.

- Duty: A legally recognized relationship between the plaintiff and defendant. The standard of care owed to trespassers is to refrain from willful, wanton, or reckless conduct. Recklessness is when one shows a conscious disregard for the rights of another.
- Breach of duty: Falling below the standard of care, or in this case, engaging in willful, wanton, or reckless conduct.
- Actual cause: Defendant must be the actual cause of the injury. Since there is only one cause in this case, the test is "but for" the defendant's conduct would the injury have occurred.
- Proximate cause: The defendant must be the proximate cause of the injury. This is tested by the foreseeability test.
- Damages: The plaintiff must have suffered harm to prevail.

Analysis

RELEVANT FACTS

- Jackie, the landlord, owes Druggie a duty because of her negligent repair.
- Druggie was breaking into the basement apartment, making him a trespasser.
- Druggie was injured by glass in the window when it gave way.

LOGICAL CONCLUSIONS AND INFERENCES

- Duty: Because Druggie was a trespasser, Jackie owed him a duty to refrain from willful, wanton, or reckless conduct.
- Breach: While Jackie may have been negligent in failing to make the repair, it does not appear that she was willful, wanton, or reckless. Therefore Druggie loses on breach of duty.
- Causation: Assuming there was a breach, but for Jackie's action Druggie would not have been injured. Also, it is foreseeable that a window with dry-rot will give way, resulting in injury.
- Damages: Druggie suffered injury when the window gave way.

Issue 3: Comparative Fault [10% of grade]

Accuracy (Rule Statement)

- Conduct on the part of the plaintiff which falls below the standard of care, which contributes to the harm.
- Comparative fault is an affirmative defense, which reduces plaintiff's recovery by the percentage of his fault.

Analysis

RELEVANT FACTS

- Druggie broke the window in the basement apartment as he was trying to get into the apartment to steal.

LOGICAL CONCLUSIONS AND INFERENCES

- Druggie contributed to his injuries by breaking the window, in an attempt to steal. This was not only unreasonable, but illegal.

Issue 4: Defamation [50% of grade]

Rule Statement

- A false statement
- published to a third party
- by the actor
- "of and concerning" the plaintiff
- tending to cause damage to plaintiff's reputation
- Opinions are not facts that can be proven or disproven, so they aren't considered false statements.
- Defamation per se: accusing someone of serious sexual misconduct.
- Defamation per quod: must prove economic harm if a per se category is not involved.
- Under the US Constitution, the status of the person or whether the statement involves a public concern can require

that the plaintiff prove malice. There is no requirement to establish malice when there is a private person in a private matter.

Analysis

RELEVANT FACTS

- Druggie posted on his Twitter account that "Jackie Oldham is an old immoral hag—she probably has dozens of cats."
- Jackie does not own any cats.
- One of Jackie's friends sees the post, and uninvites her to a party.

LOGICAL CONCLUSIONS AND INFERENCES

- Owning cats is a false statement but not defamatory.
- The issue is whether the phrase "old immoral hag" is a fact or opinion. It appears to be an opinion, but reasonable minds might differ.
- Published: Twitter counts as publication.
- Was published by Druggie about Jackie.
- Defamatory: Though a friend uninvited her to a party, the statement must hold her to scorn, ridicule, and contempt.
- Defamation per se: Accusing someone of being immoral is not necessarily accusing them of serious sexual misconduct.
- Defamation per quod: No proof of any economic harm in this case.

TORTS FINAL ISSUE SPOTTER OUTLINE

Sarah v. BRSR

1. Duty: The statute establishes the duty owed (this is NOT negligence per se)

    a. It is inappropriate to use the R.P.P. standard. The legislature has established the standard of care.
    b. Breach: Failing to follow the statute establishes breach.

        i. 420 skaters—statute requires one floor guard for "approximately" every 200 skaters.
        ii. One floor guard was ill and often not on the floor.
        iii. Skating surface: Does looking down 200 feet of floor qualify as "inspecting"?
        iv. Checking skates: Is once a year sufficient?

    c. Causation

        i. What caused the injury? Was it the wobbly wheel? Jury can make the inference.

    d. Contributory Negligence

        i. She does not remember what happened. She could have fallen herself—it was her first time skating. Also, was she negligent in not requesting another set of skates when she noticed the wobbly wheel.

Sarah v. Dr. Kildare

1. Malpractice

   a. Surgery on bruise

      i. Standard of Care: Established by custom in the profession.

         i. A U.S. practice from the 1940s does not qualify as custom today.

      ii. Damages: No indication that this surgery led to any damages.

   b. Skull removal for tumor

      i. No malpractice because it is customary to open the skull when there are signs of brain tumors.

2. Informed Consent (Patient Rule)

   a. Doctor must disclose all material risks.
   b. Sarah consented to an examination of her bruise.
   c. Exception to consent: Doctor must prove that Sarah would have consented to this if she had been awake.
   d. There was equipment about 20 minutes away that could have checked her brain in a non-evasive manner; it is unlikely she would have consented.

Peter v. Derik

1. Negligence (driving car)

   a. Duty: Derik is required to drive as a reasonably prudent person.

b. Breach: The benefit of turning around for 1 second was outweighed by the likelihood of an accident and the significant harm that could occur from a car accident.

c. Causation Actual: But for him turning around the accident would not have occurred.

d. Causation Legal: The issue is whether the bacteria in the gardening supplies was a superseding intervening event. It was not. It is foreseeable that gardening equipment might have bacteria, and the law will not relieve someone for unforeseeable extent of injury.

e. Damages

    i. Amputated arm.

    ii. Nightmares: His emotional harm is parasitic to his negligence claim.

f. Defenses: Derik might argue that Paul was negligent per se because he failed to turn on his signals. However, that negligence was not a cause of the accident.

Paramedic v. Derik

1. Firefighter's rule

    a. Has been expanded to apply to more than just firefighters. A paramedic would likely fall under this rule. Paramedic will not be able to recover.

Derik v. Beer Company

1. Negligence

    a. Duty: Status of Derik determines the duty owed. Derik was a trespasser, so the only duty is to refrain from willful and wanton conduct and to warn of traps. If Derik is a "known trespasser," then Beer Company must warn him of dangerous conditions. No duty to Derik if he is a trespasser but a duty if he is a known trespasser.

TORTS MIDTERM ISSUE SPOTTER
ESSAY OUTLINE

See if you can find the 18 possible causes of actions or affirmative defenses under these facts.

TORTS POLICY QUESTION: POSSIBLE ANSWER

The State legislature is debating the merits of contributory negligence versus pure comparative fault. Contributory negligence is the traditional common law affirmative defense to a negligence action, where any negligence by the plaintiff acts as a complete bar to plaintiff's recovery. Pure comparative faulty, in contrast, allows a partially negligent plaintiff to recover damages, reduced by their comparative fault. For the reasons discussed below, the legislature should abolish contributory negligence and adopt pure comparative fault.

Contributory negligence was created in the early 19TH century and was the primary affirmative defense until the mid-20TH century. There are several advantages to contributory negligence. One, it bars recovery to a plaintiff if they contributed, in any way, to their own injuries. And two, it is relatively easy to apply—the jury only need determine if the plaintiff was in any way at fault. The main criticism lies in that plaintiffs cannot recover for their injuries, even in situations where their negligence was very slight. For example, imagine a plaintiff who was less than 1% at fault for his injuries, which resulted in $2,000,000 in damages. The 99% at-fault defendant would not be responsible for any damages, even though they were almost completely at fault for the plaintiff's injuries.

Pure comparative fault is one answer to the inequities created by the all-or-nothing contributory negligence approach. The primary advantage to pure comparative fault is that a negligent plaintiff can recover something from the defendant, with the jury allocating fault amongst both sides. This prevents a defendant from paying nothing, even when they were partially at fault. However, one problem with pure comparative fault is that a negligent plaintiff can recover damages when they were almost exclusively at fault. Imagine for a moment a plaintiff who was 99% at fault for his injuries suing a 1% at fault defendant. Here, the plaintiff recovers 1% of the total damages.

Comparing the two systems, pure comparative fault appears more just. While on the margins both systems can create inequities, most cases are not likely in that category. The law should balance the comparative fault of both parties, which makes pure comparative fault the better system. Not always the best approach, but the best approach in almost all situations.

APPENDIX 5: STUDY OUTLINE FRAMEWORK

*From the Dukeminier Property casebook

1. First Possession: Acquisition of Property by Discovery, Capture, and Creation.

    a. Acquisition by Discovery
    b. Acquisition by Capture
    c. Acquisition by Creation

        i. Property in One's Ideas and Expressions
        ii. Property in One's Persona
        iii. Property in One's Person

2. Subsequent Possession

    a. Acquisition by Find
    b. Acquisition by Adverse Possession

        i. Elements
        ii. Mechanics
        iii. Chattels

    c. Acquisition by Gift

APPENDIX 6:
MULTIPLE-CHOICE
QUESTIONS

1. Peter and Don are high school students. As class was about to begin one day, Don thought it would be hilarious to pull the chair out from Peter as he was sitting down. Don walked over to near Peter's chair, and just as he was sitting down, Don moved the chair and Peter fell down on his rear. Peter was not harmed in any way, though he was very embarrassed as everyone in the class laughed for about a minute. What is the best tort that Peter can bring against Don?

A. Intentional Infliction of Emotional Distress

B. Assault

C. Battery

D. False Imprisonment

2. Paul purchased a new car and took it to a restaurant with valet parking. He gave the keys to Dirk, who drove the car to the parking lot across the street. Dirk decided to drive the car a couple of extra blocks because it was brand new. After parking the car, Dirk sat momentarily in the car seat, admiring the leather steering wheel cover. He then grabbed the keys from the ignition and started running the keys along the leather cover, slightly nicking the leather cover with the car keys. At the end of dinner Paul got the car and drove home, spotting the nick in the leather the next morning. If Paul files suit, will he prevail?

A. Yes, for trespass to chattels.

B. No, because there was only one small nick.

C. Yes, for conversion.

D. No, because the nick was accidental.

APPENDIX 7:
MULTIPLE-CHOICE
ANSWERS

1. The correct answer is C. A battery is the intentional contact of another in a harmful or offensive manner. The first issue is whether Don acted with intent. Don walked towards Peter's chair and desired for him to fall when he pulled it out, thereby establishing intent. Second, though Don did not directly contact Peter, he knew that by pulling out the chair it was likely that Peter's rear would contact the ground. Finally, the facts provide that Peter was not harmed. However, a battery can occur if the contact was offensive. Offensiveness is measured by what society deems as unreasonable. Here, they are in high school, and it is reasonable for a student to get embarrassed when they fall on the floor.

2. The correct answer is A. Trespass to chattels occurs when someone intentionally interferes with the chattels of another. First, Dirk knew to a substantial certainty that running the keys along the leather might scratch them, thereby establishing intent. Second, the chattel belonged to Paul. And third, a scratch qualifies as an interference.

APPENDIX 8: SAMPLE STUDY SCHEDULE

Time	Sun	Mon	Tue	Wed	Thu	Fri	Sat
6:30	Wake-up	Wake-up	Wake-up	Wake-up	Wake-up	Wake-up	Wake-up
7:00	Exercise						Exercise
7:30		Exercise	Exercise	Exercise	Exercise	Exercise	
8:00	Available						Available
8:30		Commute	Commute	Commute	Commute	Commute	
9:00		Torts	Available	Torts	Available	Torts	
9:30							Study Outline: Create, Refine, & Review
10:00	Religious Services	Available		Available		Available	
10:15		Torts Review		Torts Review		Torts Review	
10:30			Civil Procedure		Civil Procedure		
10:45		Available		Available		Available	
11:00	Available	Contracts		Contracts		Contracts	Available
11:30			Meal		Meal		

Time	Sun	Mon	Tue	Wed	Thu	Fri	Sat
Noon		Meal	Civil Procedure Review	Meal	Civil Procedure Review	Meal	
12:30	Available	Contracts Review	Class Prep	Contracts Review	Class Prep	Contracts Review	Available
1:00		Class Prep		Class Prep		Available	Available
1:30		Available	Available	Available	Available		Practice Exams
2:00		Property		Property		Property	
2:30							
3:00		Available	Legal Writing		Legal Writing	Available	
3:15		Property Review		Small Group		Property Review	
3:30	Class Prep		Available		Available		
3:45							Available
4:00		Class Prep	Class Prep	Available	Class Prep	Available	
4:30				Property Review			
5:00	Available	Commute	Commute	Commute	Commute	Commute	
5:30							
6:00	Meal	Meal	Meal	Meal	Meal	Meal	Meal

Time	Sun	Mon	Tue	Wed	Thu	Fri	Sat
6:30	Available	Available	Available	Available	Available	Relax, Fun, or Down Time	Available
7:00	Available	Class Prep	Class Prep	Class Prep	Class Prep	Relax, Fun, or Down Time	Class Prep
7:30							
8:00							
8:30							
9:00		Available	Available	Available	Available		Available
9:30		Class Prep	Class Prep	Class Prep	Class Prep	Available	Class Prep
10:00							
10:30	Unwind & Relax	Unwind & Relax	Unwind & Relax	Unwind & Relax	Unwind & Relax	Unwind & Relax	Unwind & Relax

PRIORITIZED ITEMS AS TIME ALLOWS

Class A (Must Happen)	Class B (Should Happen)	Class C (Can Skip)
Pay Bills	Reach out to friends	Social Media
Call Parents	Watch a movie	Shop for fun
Laundry	Walk in park	
Grocery Store	Read a novel	
Exercise		

ACKNOWLEDGMENTS

Writing a law school academic success book would have been impossible without my students—I learned something from each of them. My students continue to inspire me to become a better teacher, helping me understand what they need to learn the law and succeed as lawyers. If I could, I would list all their names because my success would have been impossible without each of them. Thank you for letting me learn from you.

Next, I want to thank my colleagues at the University of Idaho College of Law for their support and encouragement. Law professors generally live a solitary scholarly life, but that wasn't my experience at Idaho. David Pimentel was kind enough to share his thoughts and materials on exam design, allowing me to write a more balanced chapter on law school exams. Then there is Samuel Newton, who helped me understand the need for law students to spend time on their inward journey. A special thank you to my colleague Wendy Gerwick Couture, who led the faculty summer writing group. Without her leadership this book would have taken me much longer to complete. Then there is Ashley Cease, who on her second day on the job at Idaho provided insight into the inward journey section of the book. The original title I created for the book was dreadful, so thank you to my colleague Karen Wellman for her complete candor and honesty in revealing this to me.

Finally, let me thank a few others who helped me on my journey. Alexander Baez, my brother, used his years of marketing experience with the Coca-Cola company to help develop a new title for the book. Jessica Heitzinger and Clayton Boeckel, my research assistants, went above and beyond by finding useful material and exposing gaps in my knowledge, which led me to modify my views on a few topics. Mark Matthews, a former colleague, provided me with meaningful feedback on my manuscript. And thank you to Autumn Smith, a practicing lawyer and recent law school graduate, for helping me understand some of the disability challenges facing law students and the difficulties they have in getting accommodations. Last but not least, thank you to each person in my "student stories." Each of you made an impact on my teaching and how I interact with students today.

ABOUT THE AUTHOR

P rofessor H. Beau Baez is on the faculty at Ohio Northern University Claude Pettit College of Law. He began his teaching career in 2000 and has taught thousands of students at seven law schools. In addition, he has worked one-on-one with law students at many law schools in the United States, the United Kingdom, Canada, and Australia. Courses he has taught include Torts, Tax, Business Associations, Wills & Trusts, Contracts, Civil Procedure, Legal Writing, and Criminal Procedure.

In addition to teaching, Professor Baez is a YouTube creator at YouTube.com/LearnLawBetter This is the first popular channel hosted by a law professor, with videos now viewed millions of times and subscribers in over 150 countries. A prolific author, he has written several books and numerous scholarly articles. Also, he has an academic success blog for law students at LearnLawBetter.com

His four undergraduate degrees are in the fields of Speech Communications, Accounting, and Religion. At Georgetown University he earned the JD and LLM (tax) degrees. After law school, he practiced law for eight years with the Multistate Tax Commission in Washington, DC. At the Commission he administered a successful voluntary compliance program and assisted in preparing briefs before State supreme courts and the United States Supreme Court—he has attended more than a hundred oral arguments at the Supreme Court.

When not working, he enjoys taking long hikes, enjoying the natural beauty around him.

ADDITIONAL RESOURCES

Resource	*URL*
Website	LearnLawBetter.com
Academic Success Blog	LearnLawBetter.com/law-school-tips
YouTube Channel	YouTube.com/LearnLawBetter
Facebook	Facebook.com/LearnLawBetter
Instagram	Instagram.com/LearnLawBetter
LinkedIn	LinkedIn.com/company/LearnLawBetter